THE SOCIALLY INTELLIGENT PROJECT MANAGER

THE SOCIALLY INTELLIGENT PROJECT MANAGER*

Soft Skills That
Prevent Hard Days

---

*BECAUSE ONE UNHAPPY PERSON
CAN RUIN YOUR BEAUTIFUL PLAN.

KIM WASSON, PMP

Interior Illustrations by Stephen L. Wasson

BK®

Berrett–Koehler Publishers, Inc.

Berrett-Koehler Publishers, Inc.
1333 Broadway, Suite 1000
Oakland, CA 94612-1921
Tel: (510) 817-2277
Fax: (510) 817-2278
www.bkconnection.com

ORDERING INFORMATION
Quantity sales. Special discounts are available on quantity purchases by corporations, associations, and others. For details, contact the "Special Sales Department" at the Berrett-Koehler address above.
Individual sales. Berrett-Koehler publications are available through most bookstores. They can also be ordered directly from Berrett-Koehler: Tel: (800) 929-2929; Fax: (802) 864-7626; www.bkconnection.com.
Orders for college textbook / course adoption use. Please contact Berrett-Koehler: Tel: (800) 929-2929; Fax: (802) 864-7626.

Distributed to the U.S. trade and internationally by Penguin Random House Publisher Services.

Berrett-Koehler and the BK logo are registered trademarks of Berrett-Koehler Publishers, Inc.

Printed in the United States of America.

Berrett-Koehler books are printed on long-lasting acid-free paper. When it is available, we choose paper that has been manufactured by environmentally responsible processes. These may include using trees grown in sustainable forests, incorporating recycled paper, minimizing chlorine in bleaching, or recycling the energy produced at the paper mill.

Library of Congress Cataloging-in-Publication Data

Names: Wasson, Kim, author.
Title: The socially intelligent project manager : soft skills that prevent hard days / Kim Wasson, PMP.
Description: First edition. | Oakland, CA : Berrett-Koehler Publishers, [2020] | Includes bibliographical references and index.
Identifiers: LCCN 2019031880 | ISBN 9781523087105 (paperback) | ISBN 9781523087112 (pdf) | ISBN 9781523087129 (epub)
Subjects: LCSH: Project management. | Teams in the workplace—Training of. | Soft skills.
Classification: LCC HD69.P75 W374 2020 | DDC 658.4/04—dc23
LC record available at https://lccn.loc.gov/2019031880

First Edition
28 27 26 25 24 23 22 21 20   10 9 8 7 6 5 4 3 2 1

Set in Electra LT Std Regular by Westchester Publishing Services
Cover designer: Susan Malikowski, DesignLeaf Studio
Cover illustration: Lisa Haney

With thanks to my patient husband, Tris,
who has sat through every major presentation
I've ever made (often multiple times) without complaint
and who has given me endless encouragement.

CONTENTS

CONTENTS

INTRODUCTION

We've all had those days when we leave work thinking "if people would just DO THEIR JOBS this project would be fine." (Every day was one of those when I was a new project manager, in fact.) Of course, if it were that easy, no one would need project managers. Projects run on people, and that's where most of the work of project management lies.

In 1995, Daniel Goleman wrote a book on emotional intelligence. It was the seminal work on the subject—part behavioral psychology, part neurology—and has been used in many different fields by many different kinds of practitioners. The book itself was a definition of the term "emotional intelligence," which is a little unwieldy for a quick reference. Wikipedia has a nice definition though: "the capability of individuals to recognize their own emotions and those of others, discern between different feelings and label them appropriately, use emotional information to guide thinking and behavior, and manage and/or adjust emotions to adapt to environments or achieve one's goal(s)."[1]

It sounds squishy and hard to work with, but there's real science on our side when it comes to the people side of projects. We can use that science to help keep projects in "just fine" territory.

A dozen years after publishing *Emotional Intelligence,* Dr. Goleman followed it with a new book, *Social Intelligence.* After further research both behavioral and neurological, *Social Intelligence* took on the same material from a different viewpoint. While much of emotional intelligence is introspective, social intelligence is more about collaboration and continued interaction with others. In other words, the connections.

For project managers the translation of all this is that to really be effective we need to understand what makes the people we work with tick, communicate effectively with them based on that understanding, and help them connect with each other. It's a tall order, but it's critical to project success.

Because one unhappy person can ruin your beautiful plan.

A BALANCING ACT

Project management is a balancing act. We need to constantly balance people with process, common goals with individual goals, and immediate progress with sustained improvement. It's a lot to manage.

Dealing with the people side of the equation can be like nailing Jell-O to a tree: it changes from minute to minute; it's slippery and wiggles around a lot. Those days of wishing everyone would just do what you tell them happen a lot more to people who focus only on the process side of the work and largely ignore the people side. If you're a process aficionado, emotional and social intelligence concepts and tools can help make the people side of the equation more process-like and easier to get your arms around. If you love the people side and enjoy the challenge of understanding and connecting with people, these concepts can put a few more tools in your project management toolbox.

WHY SHOULD I CARE?

Any project is largely dependent on the people working on it. The people landscape changes constantly, and without a solid basis it's hard to keep up. Over my career, the more projects I worked on and the more management positions I held, the fewer people I encountered who were actually lazy or incompetent (not that there haven't been some of those, but they're really the minority). People didn't do their job because they had other priorities, had other work on their plate, were unmotivated, or were overloaded. Their understanding of their job was not necessarily the same as my understanding of their job, and their priorities were not always the same as mine.

I found that the more I connected with people and talked in a language they understood, the more attention they paid to what I had to say. Everyone is busy, and everyone has their own priorities. By using emotional and social intelligence tools, you can help make your priorities theirs too.

At this point you're probably wondering what exactly I bring to the party. The answer is that I'm, um, seasoned (well seasoned even). I've been doing this stuff (project management and management) a long time. I've made just about every mistake you can make, and I've had to deal with the aftermath. As a result, I've built my toolkit with things that can help me avoid making those mistakes a second time. At one time or another I've pulled out and applied every tool and concept I'll show you, and I can testify that each and every one works. I've put examples of problems and techniques—true stories— throughout. Every true story really happened to or around me. Some of them are good examples and some are cautionary tales, but you'll see why the longer I'm at this, the better I understand how important the people side of project management is to project success.

My background is in software development. I've worked just about every piece of the process, from coding to quality assurance (QA) to management to project management, using processes from Water-fall to eXtreme Programming to Agile to Kanban, so most (but not all) of my true stories are from the world of software. The social intelligence tools in this book work as well in construction, event planning, and any other project management arena as they do in the world of software development, so please don't be put off by the examples if you're not developing software. (If you think about it as you read, I'll bet you have plenty of your own true stories that fit right into the framework already.)

CATS AND DOGS AND HORSES—OH MY!

Submitted for your consideration: cats, dogs, and horses as paradigms for managing teams.

Cats are generally solitary, self-sufficient, competitive with other cats, and independent. We've all heard the saying that project management is like herding cats: it's hard to get them all going the same direction, and as soon as you do, one wanders off and you have to start over. That's the starting point with a new team. Without social or emotional intelligence you'll spend a lot of time cat herding.

Horses are herd animals. Their survival depends on cooperation, they read nonverbal cues exceptionally well, and they're very social. Their awareness of the connections within their herd (and with humans) is the very definition of social intelligence, so there are a lot of lessons to be learned from the world of horses. (For the dog people among us, dogs are similar to horses in many ways, being pack animals.)

Humans are a mixture of all these characteristics—sometimes cooperative, sometimes competitive, sometimes social, sometimes independent. Understanding where each person is, and where the team (our herd!) is on the continuum (or even on a certain day), knowing how to manage the cues, and being able to move from herding cats to leading the pack are the real purpose—and reward—for using social intelligence in projects.

STRAIGHT FROM THE HORSE'S MOUTH: A STARTER TOOL

I've learned a few important social intelligence lessons from natural horsemanship, all of which I apply pretty much daily in my project management work. (There's a true intersection between these two; it's not just another horse person finding a reason to talk horses.)

The first lesson: the more I listen, the more my horse "talks." This is absolutely as true of people as it is of horses. You'll learn more from asking a leading question and letting someone tell you what's on her mind than you ever will in a status meeting or from a status report. The more comfortable people are with you, the more honest they'll be and the more information they'll provide.

It's easy (okay, easier) when you have the right tools. Nothing has to be touchy-feely, but the people side does take just as much, if not more, attention than the process side. In fact, we're going to take it a step at a time. Each step builds on the one before. The flowchart in figure 1 shows what the whole thing looks like.

So with that, away we go.

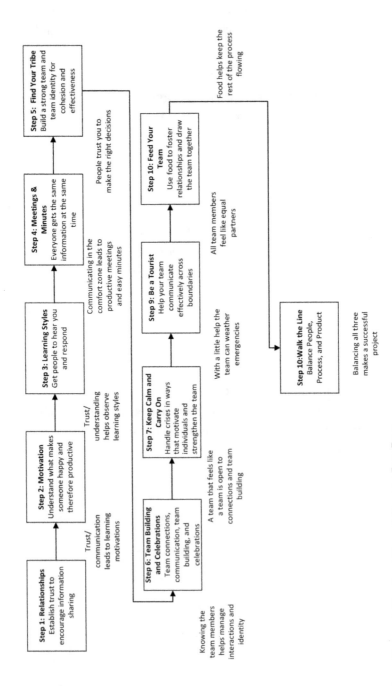

Figure 1 The Road Map: 10 Steps to Easy Days

BUILD SOME BRIDGES

Why Don't People Tell Me Things?

You have your team. You have your project. You've set all the project parameters and work has started. You get to the first milestone, and that day your team tells you they'll miss it. They have blockers, they're working on it, they're *sure* it will be done tomorrow . . . or the next day.

Now you're frustrated. They *knew* the schedule. Why didn't they give you some warning? You could have gotten them some help or at least let management know the schedule was at risk. It's gonna look bad (and it's gonna be bad).

Does this sound familiar?

No one likes to give bad news, so people tend to avoid bringing up problems whenever possible (especially if they think it's going to get ugly in the telling). They'll procrastinate and hope the problem will solve itself, they'll hide the information, and ultimately they may try to blame someone else. People don't tell you things if they don't trust you. For project managers this can be deadly; we run on up-to-the-minute information. No one likes project surprises. So how do you get people to trust you?

There really are no shortcuts to gaining that critical trust from your team. All your nice Gantt charts and burndown analyses aren't going to help with this task. You have to put in the time and establish relationships. This sounds both difficult and slippery, but there *is* a process to support what is admittedly the art of building relationships. That's the good news. The bad news is that it's not one and done; once you establish a relationship you have to maintain it.

You need to build relationships with people on your team one at a time and one-on-one. Relationships don't happen in project meetings, they don't happen in team events, and they don't happen on demand. You'll have to do this in person with every person on the team.

We're not talking about BFFs-who-go-out-and-have-a-beer relationships here. You don't have to go overboard, and you don't have to spend nonworking time with everyone on your team (or anyone, really). You just have to create a professional relationship built on mutual respect and trust with each person on your team. It doesn't stop with your team, either. Everyone you interact with on a project deserves attention. Your suppliers, your management, your support staff—having cordial relationships with them doesn't just mean they think you're a nice guy. It means that they're willing to listen to what you have to say, they'll put you ahead in their queue when you need something, and they'll work with you to get things done. Your project success depends on this.

If you've worked with some (or all) of your team members before and have a good working relationship with each, you can just skip ahead to the care and feeding, Step 9. If, however, you haven't worked with some or all of the people on the team or you have a poor relationship with any of them, you'll need to get busy on the bridge building.

SUBTLE BIAS

Establishing a connection starts with understanding your own position, including what you've heard about someone and your basic beliefs (emotional intelligence stuff). One of the biggest barriers to building a relationship and gaining trust is subtle bias. Not the big stuff like religion, about which most people are pretty self-aware, but the small stuff like the way someone dresses or someone's age. Before you start relationship building, be sure you do some self-examination to identify any preferences on your part, and then pay attention later to combat any bias that might get in the way of the connections you need to make.

TRY IT

Let's try an exercise (sorry to the folks who prefer visuals).

You are managing a large commercial building project and need to engage a structural engineer, a landscape architect, an archaeologist, and a construction manager. You have two candidates for each position sitting in your waiting room, and you haven't seen the résumés (they were screened by the Human Resources Department). Who do you pick?

Structural Engineer Candidates

Candidate A, Carolina	Candidate B, Carlos
• *Fairly young* • *Professionally dressed (suit, skirt, heels)* • *Female*	• *Middle aged* • *Dressed in jeans and a flannel shirt* • *Carrying a hardhat* • *Male*

Landscape Architect Candidates

Candidate C, Joan	Candidate D, John
• *Middle aged* • *Wearing gardening clothes* • *Dirt under her fingernails* • *Has an air of certainty* • *Female*	• *Young* • *Dressed in a sharp suit* • *Carrying his laptop* • *Male*

Archaeologist Candidates

Candidate E, Brandie	Candidate F, Bob
• *Early 20s* • *Casually dressed* • *Laptop in hand* • *Female*	• *A bit older than middle aged, gray hair and beard* • *Dressed informally in khakis, boots, and a somewhat disreputable hat* • *Male*

Construction Manager Candidates

Candidate G, Harry	Candidate H, Hattie
• *Middle aged* • *White shirt* • *Hardhat in hand* • *Male*	• *Middle aged* • *Wearing a suit* • *On her cell phone (puts it down when you enter the room)* • *Female*

Who did you pick? I asked you to pick based on appearance because most people count on first impressions more than you'd think, and this first impression based on appearance can carry through to deciding who is the best fit for your team. Turn the page for the choices most people make (in my experience presenting this information).

ANSWER

- Structural Engineer: Most people choose Carlos (B) over Carolina (A). In their minds, he looks the part and they assume he has more experience.
- Landscape Architect: Most people pick Joan (C) over John (D), since she seems to be quite experienced with plants.
- Archaeologist: Most people pick candidate Bob (F) over Brandie (E). He definitely looks the part of an archaeologist; they can just picture him on a dig.
- Construction Manager: Choice of Harry (G) or Hattie (H) tend to be evenly divided, according to people's prior experience with project managers.

Now let's try it again with some résumé and background information.

Structural Engineer Candidates

Candidate A, Carolina	Candidate B, Carlos
• *Fairly young* • *Professionally dressed (suit, skirt, heels)* • *Female* • **Harvard graduate** • **Certified** • **Wealth of large-structure** experience • **Her services are in high demand, but she has an opening right now** • **Widely trusted in the local industry**	• *Middle aged* • *Dressed in jeans and a flannel shirt* • *Carrying a hardhat* • *Male* • **Broad hands-on construction experience** • **Certified** • **Experience is primarily residential**

Landscape Architect Candidates

Candidate C, Joan	Candidate D, John
• *Middle aged* • *Wearing gardening clothes* • *Dirt under her fingernails* • *Has an air of certainty* • *Female* • **Master gardener** • **Excellent troubleshooter** • **Typically advises on individual plant placement and health**	• *Young* • *Dressed in a sharp suit* • *Carrying his laptop* • *Male* • **Skilled designer** • **Produces plans and visuals for review and approval** • **Manages design implementation**

Archaeologist Candidates

Candidate E, Brandie	Candidate F, Bob
• *Early 20s* • *Casually dressed* • *Laptop in hand* • *Female* • **Parents were archaeologists, so has a lifetime of experience on digs** • *PhD in archaeology* • *Excellent research skills* • *Known for being very pragmatic*	• *A bit older than middle aged, gray hair and beard* • *Dressed informally in khakis, boots, and a somewhat disreputable hat* • *Male* • *First career was as a college professor* • **Recently embarked on a second career as an archaeologist** • **Has been on a few digs and has taken college archaeology courses**

Construction Manager Candidates

Candidate G, Harry	Candidate H, Hattie
• *Middle aged* • *White shirt* • *Hardhat in hand* • *Male* • **Wealth of hands-on experience** • **Significant construction management experience** • **Likes to be on-site, discussing and inspecting**	• *Middle aged* • *Wearing a suit* • *On her cell phone (puts it down when you enter the room)* • *Female* • **Excellent project management skills** • **Significant construction management experience**

Did you change any of your choices based on this information? Often people don't ask detailed questions in interviews because they're already leaning toward one candidate based on appearance, demeanor, or assumptions.

ANSWER

With this full knowledge I would choose the following:

- Structural Engineer: Carolina (A). I want the person with large-structure experience who is known in the industry. Carlos's (B) hands-on experience is good, but age isn't a predictor of performance (in either direction; I work in tech and the age bias there is toward younger people), and John doesn't have the large-structure experience.
- Landscape Architect: John (D). Joan (C) might be called in for another role, but for a landscape architect I need to have a view of the final product.
- Archaeologist: Brandie (D) has the skills and background I need. Bob (F) is a newbie and isn't likely to be able to do the work I need, even if he does look like the movie rendition of an archaeologist.
- Construction Manager: Harry (G) and Hattie (H) are a toss-up for me; it would depend on the situation, the rest of the team, and the soft skills (we'll get to all that in a later step).

So what influences those initial choices? Clothing, gender, and age can all be subtle biases if we aren't looking for them. The bias is not necessarily generic but can be based on expectations or previous experience. We have an idea of how the person filling this role should look.

Many people are influenced by the suit John (Landscape Architect) is wearing, as well as his age, equating experience with plants with the ability to imagine and present a consolidated vision.

Many people head right for Bob, the guy who looks like an older Indiana Jones. That's the general expectation for an archaeologist, the vision we have in our minds.

In a position like the one I'm staffing, there's often a gender bias toward men when considering Harry and Hattie, candidates for construction manager. The hardhat seems to be an influencing factor as well.

ESTABLISHING A RELATIONSHIP

If you haven't worked with a team member before, you need to start your relationship from scratch. That means that anything you've heard about how easy or difficult the person is to work with can't color your approach. You really don't have any idea of circumstances that might have made someone else form an opinion of a team member—and remember, you're good at this. Even if someone else had a bad experience, you'll put in the time to have a good one. It's always good to be informed (we are, after all, collectors, analysts, and disseminators of information), but don't prejudge.

There are a number of methods of building a relationship, which I'll cover in general descending order of effectiveness:

1. Stop by

    If the person is anywhere within easy reach, stop by her desk or work area. Don't make her come to you. When you stop by be sure it isn't always for something project related. If you only bring tasks and questions people are going to run when they see you coming. Take a walk to the coffee machine, ask how her weekend went, ask what you might be able to do to help her. Let the person know you're there to help and to run interference to get obstacles out of her way. Find something you have in common. Do this regularly—not on a schedule (that becomes obvious pretty quickly and seems disingenuous), but when you're in the area or when you haven't talked one-on-one for a while. Don't use up a whole lot of her time; just make contact and start (or work on) the relationship.

    One caveat to this is that if every time you stop by you see the person's shoulders start creeping up to their ears, stopping by (at least at first) is not going to work well, or you've started with the wrong topic. Some people just cringe at interruptions or informal person-to-person communication. Set up a meeting instead.

2. Schedule meetings

If stopping by doesn't work, you can rely on regular meetings. Even if stopping by works well, meetings are an excellent forum for maintaining your relationship.

I usually schedule a one-on-one meeting with each person on my team either weekly or every two weeks. It can be as short as half an hour. Yes, I know this sounds insane and like a huge time sink, but it pays off. This is not a meeting where I grill people or ask them to recite status. It's their time. I don't let them cancel a meeting because they have nothing to talk about. I have yet to have a regular meeting with anyone on my team when there really wasn't anything on his mind. When you do this, keep a list of leading questions so that if the person doesn't come in with topics, you're not sitting in silence (it's not a police interrogation after all). Ask how he's feeling about the project or his work. Ask if anyone or anything is getting in his way. That will usually break the ice, and things that are on someone's mind come up in the conversation.

Remember not to panic or react negatively in this meeting. If you need to call someone on the carpet for something, schedule a different meeting. This one is all about building and maintaining trust. You will get a huge amount of information from each person. You'll be able to help find solutions to problems. Perhaps most importantly you'll be able to connect the dots— see if there are patterns in what the team members are telling you, see where one team member might be able to help another, and get a good view of the team's dynamics.

These meetings are a good way to get started, although establishing a connection by stopping by is usually a better first contact—it makes the meetings a bit less overwhelming or scary (or annoying) for the team members. They're an excellent way to maintain the relationship.

3. Videoconference

If you're located in the same area as the team member, videoconferencing is silly, but it's really valuable if you're trying to establish and maintain a relationship with someone in another location. If possible, it's really best to visit the other location at the beginning of a project for many reasons, not the least of which is that it's much easier to establish relationships in person. While you're there you can spend time informally with team members during dinners, outings, etc.

For sustaining the relationship, though, videoconferencing on a regular basis is really helpful. It helps to have visual cues (is she frowning when she's telling you something?) and to keep you from being just a voice on the phone.

4. Make calls (VOIP or phone, there's no difference)

Making calls usually doesn't make sense if you're in the same general physical location, but for distributed teams, calls will help maintain the relationship. (The Vice President of Engineering at one company I worked for had a theory that the half-life of face-to-face contact is six months. I've found that generally true, so be sure to supplement the calls at least with video occasionally.) During a voice call you'll have to listen for pauses in odd places, tone of voice, and other auditory cues. Have those calls regularly, and run them the same way as the face-to-face meetings.

5. Use Instant Messaging

Instant Messaging (Skype, Slack, etc.) is pretty low on the totem pole of useful relationship management and useless for initially establishing a relationship, but it does have the benefit of being reasonably two way. It's a good supplement for other methods because it's quick and you can do it quite often without disturbing anyone. Make full use of emoticons and be sure to follow up with regular meetings.

6. Send email

Email is worse than useless for establishing and maintaining relationships. It's one-way communication, open to interpretation, and without any way to read immediate reaction. Be very cautious with email in general for all these reasons.

True Story *I worked on a big, multiyear project with a team located primarily in the United States but with an integrated outsourced team in Romania. My first month or two was really rocky, to the point where the Romanian project manager didn't want to work with me. I went there (for a single day!), spent the whole day with her, shared meals (see Step 9), met the rest of the team, and really established an excellent relationship. One day was all it took for us to get comfortable. We worked together for years and still keep in touch.*

REPAIRING A RELATIONSHIP

If you've had a rocky time with someone on your team during previous projects, you'll have to undo that damage before you can establish a better relationship. Fixing relationships that went off the rails in previous projects is a top priority for many reasons, not the least of which is that the person on the other end of the relationship is likely to talk to other team members about how hard you can be to work with. If that happens, you'll have a lot of untangling to do, so best to get started fixing the problem immediately.

The first thing to do is a postmortem (okay, in politically correct terms, a "retrospective") on your previous dealings with this team member. (That is, on your own, take a look at how things went before.) What are the root causes of the issues? What went well in the course of the project? What can you improve and how? You really need to focus on yourself and not the other person. You can't control another person's behavior, but you can control your own reactions. Walking into a conciliatory meeting armed with how the other person can change is not going to get you into a better relationship. Generally, admitting to any issues you caused (and there are going to be some, if only in the way you reacted to a situation or discussion) opens up the conversation on how to work better together.

Armed with this self-analysis, meet with the team member. Start with an acknowledgment that your previous relationship could have been better. Talk about the positives: where and how you thought the two of you connected or worked well together. Then talk about what you think *you* can do (right out of your self-review) to make it better this time around. Recognize what this person does well—technical skills, soft skills, whatever it is. Remember that everyone is good at something; it's your job to figure out what that something is. (I'll have more about this in a later step and another context, but it's also useful for building relationships.) Ask for the other person's opinion and really listen.

When you start with what went well, it puts the entire discussion on a different trajectory. When you talk about what you yourself can do better, it disarms defensiveness.

Find some common ground. Remember, you're not trying to be best friends. You're trying to establish and maintain a good, cordial, productive working relationship. We don't always like everyone we work with, but we're grownups and can certainly get along with everyone.

MAINTAINING RELATIONSHIPS

So now you have a good working relationship with every member of your team. How do you keep it up?

We've talked about one-on-one meetings. Keep those regular meetings with every team member. Make the meetings that person's time, and don't cancel the meetings because there's nothing to talk about.

Touch base with people regularly. Stop by briefly or say hello in the hallway and ask how things are going and if the team member needs anything from you. It doesn't take a lot of time, and it keeps you in the loop between meetings. You can do the same via Instant Messaging with team members in other locations.

Talk about things other than work. Avoid hot topics (politics and religion, as always) and don't get too personal, but even a quick exchange about the weather can keep communications more relaxed.

Use all the communication channels at your disposal to be sure you check in with your team members.

Establishing trust is important, but trust is a two-way street. While your team members are learning to trust you, you need to be able to trust them as well. Part of this is up to them—they have to actually be trustworthy. A lot of it is under your control, though. Unless it will torpedo the project, start from a position of trust. Don't make a team member justify every estimate or statement; trust him to do the job he was hired (or volunteered) to do. Be approachable; if there's a problem, you want people to come to you with it right away, not fear for their job if they have an issue. If a team member does something that seems to violate the trust, do your best to figure out why it happened. (If someone misses dates, she could be overly optimistic, and you will need to add contingency and get her some help with estimating. If someone has other assignments on her plate, you need to know what they are and get some relative priorities so the estimates are more accurate or so you can petition for adjustment of the priorities.)

Finally, don't be too quick to offer solutions. As project managers, we spend a lot of time figuring out how to solve problems or how to do things better, but sometimes people are coming to you just to talk or vent. Before you interrupt with how someone might solve a problem or make a situation better, ask if the person wants advice or just wants to let you know what's going on.

A HIERARCHY OF RELATIONSHIPS

Some teams are really too big for you to be able to establish a relationship with every team member (I've had 300-member teams, for example, spread across four locations in three countries). In a very large team you probably just want to try to recognize the names of all the team members and know what group they're working in.

For this kind of project, you generally have a group of team leads or managers that you work with. Be sure to establish a relationship with each member of this core team in the usual way.

One of the difficulties with a large team like this is that the information you get from your core team is only as good as the information they get from their own teams, no matter how strong your relationship with the core team members. That means you want these core team members to establish the same kind of trust with their own teams that you've created with them. The way they do that may vary from culture to culture, although the channels are the same.

Encourage those relationships by asking leading questions, questions your core team members will only be able to answer if they're working well with their own teams. Questions like "How's your team feeling about the schedule?" and "What blockers are your people running into?" and "What's the stress level like on your team?" as well as the usual questions about risk, schedule, and progress will encourage them to build relationships with their own teams. Never underestimate the impact of leading by example. If you work hard at establishing and maintaining relationships with the core team, you'll demonstrate both the value and the methods for paying it forward.

NOT JUST FOR TEAMS

Now that you know how to build and maintain relationships with the individuals on your team it's time to broaden your view.

Of course, your team is the most important set of people with whom you need good working relationships, but there are other people who can make or break your project. Some of these people are specific to projects you're working on; others are going to pop up again and again in different projects you take on. Both are important.

Take some time to identify those key people outside your team. If you're running a software project, that might include people from a Database Administration or Operations group, for example. Be sure you've got the right person. The right person might be the one who gives (and enforces) instructions and assignments, but that's not al-ways the case. Your key contacts are the people who can get things done for you, either because they're experts, because they're at the right place in the chain of command, or because they're well respected and well liked among their peers. After you've identified these key contacts, put them on your relationship list and start build-ing. You're going to need to work a little harder both to build the relationship in the first place and then to maintain it because you often won't have daily interactions with these key contacts and probably won't have regular meetings with them. Take a look at Step 9 and see if you can use some food to enhance the relationship (take them to lunch or out to coffee). We all get busy and can let time slip away from us, so think about setting some reminders on your calendar to touch base with each of your key contacts. That way you're not only reaching out when you need something from them. Be sure to reciprocate as well—help your key contacts out whenever you can.

TRY IT

You run an operations group. You rotate technical experts through your support and operations departments for assistance as on-call support (when there's an issue, there's an expert to call in for advice and support).

You've assigned one of your best people to work a weekend shift as that next line of defense. He's gotten you out of numerous jams in the past and you trust him completely based on that track record.

During that weekend shift there's a critical system problem. The operations support team calls your expert. He doesn't answer or get back to the team for four hours. During that period of time the team calls you for help. In those hours you frantically look for someone available right now who can help. The recovery is botched but eventually completed, causing you to miss your service-level commitment.

You are not happy. How do you respond?

PART 2

What you didn't know, but would have if you'd established a relationship and the associated trust, is that your expert has a child who recently developed a chronic and serious medical condition. He had to take his child to the emergency room during the shift. (Like many things that affect your project's success, this isn't something you'd think—or want—to ask. The trust has to be there for the person to volunteer the information.)

What might you have done differently if you had known?

(Some possible actions: assigned him as a backup only, or assigned a backup to him in case he wasn't available, or not assigned him at all to off-shift work until the medical issue is resolved.)

As you can see from "Part 2," maintaining a relationship has immediate and important benefits. It's always worth the effort.

STEP 2

ASK "WHO'S YOUR HERO?"

One Unmotivated Person Can Ruin Your Beautiful Plan

We all know that one unmotivated person can ruin your beautiful plan. You need to uncover each team member's motivations and try to satisfy those motivations within the limits of your project.

There's just one little thing: how in the world do you figure that out, and what do you do with the information once you have it?

It's not always easy to ferret out what motivates people, but there are some tools and tricks that can help. (And since you've already established relationships with the members of your team, you have a good basis to start work on the motivation puzzle.)

UNCOVERING MOTIVATION

The cardinal rule of discovering motivation is to not assume that everyone is motivated by what makes you happy personally. There are as many motivators as there are people.

One way to figure out what motivates someone is to just ask her. It sounds easy, but unless you have established a good relationship with her (more specifically, unless she trusts you with what she's going to tell you) you might not get very far. Not only that, sometimes people aren't really all that clear on their own motivations and will tell you what's on their minds at that particular moment. It's useful information but often incomplete.

You can start a discussion with some options. Management 3.0 sells a pack of motivation cards that can help, and the cards make the whole process a bit more informal.[1] Packs have only 10 cards, so you may want to supplement them or use them in a way that allows the person you're working with to add their own. You can have people sort them, rank them, put them into piles, or whatever works. (Or make your own cards, depending on what motivates you.)

"What makes you want to come to work in the morning?" is a good question to ask. Assuming there's *something* at work that interests the person, her answer should be revealing with respect to what motivates her. (If she can't think of anything, you already have an unmotivated person on your hands. Try asking, "What's your dream job?" instead. Follow up with questions about what makes the job she mentioned a dream job and then see what elements of that dream you can bring to her current work.)

Another good way to figure out what motivates someone is to ask how his weekend went. On weekends people typically do things that they enjoy and they aren't shy about sharing. If someone likes downhill skiing, adrenaline is probably a motivator (so you might have a deadline performer). If someone likes playing chess, you might look at strategic options or discussions to motivate him. See where this is going?

True Story *I was a new manager at a large corporation during an economic downturn. Hiring from outside the company was almost impossible, especially for supporting functions, so the company ran retraining programs for proven performers who wanted to move into a new career area. Programming was one of the biggest retraining efforts. I needed a programmer for my department and found the perfect person who had just come out of the retraining. George had been a very high performer in his previous position, someone to whom* *everyone came for help. He had gotten bored in that position and was very clear in telling me that what he needed now was a new challenge. That was his motivation for the retraining. I happily moved George into a position where he could learn the ropes without having to deal much with our internal clients. The learning curve was a bit steep, but it was clear he was up to the task. Within months, George was failing. He'd drag into work, had trouble finishing assignments, and was very unhappy. I was getting a lot of pressure to reassign George and bring on someone else, but I just couldn't shake the feeling that I was missing something. I looked carefully at what he'd done before and at what he'd told me when I interviewed him, and I decided to restructure the job. In the restructuring, he moved to a somewhat less difficult programming assignment with a lot more client contact. (As a plus, I had another programmer who was getting tired of babysitting that particular client and was happy to pick up the work George had been doing.) Within weeks George was a superstar again, happy and productive. All of which is to say that people are complicated beings and they don't always know what motivates them. Even when someone tells you what gets them moving, be sure to check back after you provide that motivation.*

THE POWER OF HEROES

You can tell a lot about what motivates people by the heroes who impress them.

True Story *I got my master's degree while I was working, so I spent several years doing various not-specifically-work-related research projects. One of these had to do with creativity, and I managed to get an interview with James Gosling (inventor of the Java programming language) as research. I put the interview on my calendar and took off work for an hour to do the interview. Imagine my surprise when I got back to work and a group of Gen X software engineers (who were really not impressed by anything) was waiting for me. They* *literally sat on the carpet in my office to ask questions about the great man.*

I'd been working with these engineers for months, so I already had a pretty good handle on what motivated them. Their interest in James Gosling confirmed that they wanted to turn their world on its ear. They wanted to be like James Gosling, running on the bleeding edge of technology. The strength of their reaction, however, took me by surprise and got me thinking about what parts of this experience I might be able to apply more generally. The experience spawned an exercise that I call The Power of Heroes. For a group, The Power of Heroes exercise is a great icebreaker; for an individual, it's a really good way to uncover someone's true passion. Simply ask, "Who's your hero?" (For people uncomfortable with that question, you can ask, "Who do you admire most?" but don't limit the answer to real people.) Even the difference between preferring Batman to Superman can tell you a lot. (Prefer Batman? My experience has been that it's because Batman has no superpowers unless you count wealth. He does it all himself. Batman lovers often want justice but prefer to pull themselves up by their bootstraps. Give them a task, offer whatever resources are available, and get out of their way. Superman, on the other hand, has plenty of superpowers and could surely take over the world, but he prefers to work incognito for the benefit of humanity. Superman lovers often like to do the most good and are happy without too much fuss about it. If you have anything that will better anyone's lot, from applications to improved tools within the group, these folks are likely to be happy to help. These aren't always the reasons, but they're a great way to start.) Follow up with the "why"—the reasons I've given above are often the motivators, but not always. I did this exercise with a friend recently and followed up with "Why Superman?" The reason was Superman's strength. This led to further discussion that had to do more with excellence at your craft and recognition of that excellence by others, and even to a discussion of real-life heroes who manage work-life balance well. You never know where the discussion is going to lead.

THERE MUST BE *SOME* MOTIVATORS
I CAN LOOK FOR

There are indeed some common motivators. You'll run into these fairly often, so put some tools in your toolkit to satisfy them.

First, a list (so you can use it as a cheat sheet to get started):

- Recognition
- Rewards
- Money
- Challenge
- Competition
- Learning
- Teaching
- Time off
- Trust

This is a pretty basic set of motivators that you can look for before you do a deep dive. Remember, though, that they manifest in different ways, and usually people have more than one thing they're looking for out of life (and the job, and the project . . .).

I have yet to work with anyone who doesn't want some kind of **recognition**. This can be tricky, though, because some people really don't like *public* recognition. For those people, praise in front of their peers can be demotivating. Watch people's reactions to public praise (of them or of others) to get a clue about whether public recognition is welcome. Praise one-on-one, however, is rarely a problem. Use it wisely and be sure it's warranted, otherwise your recognition won't mean anything. Don't hesitate to give credit where credit is due. This works with individuals as well as with an entire team. Recognizing a team member's work or effort to that person's manager (if that manager isn't you) is an excellent motivator and will help the manager as well. If your team member likes public recognition, you don't have to make a big deal out of it. For example, in your regular team meeting announce, "Annette came up with this great improvement to our process. We're going to start using it for the whole team." (If Annette likes to present or teach, you can hand the meeting over to her to talk about the change for further motivation points.)

Project managers are pretty good at giving **rewards** at the end of a project, but for those motivated by rewards there are lots of ways of providing small, interim rewards for work well done. These can be geared toward the work at hand—such as a battery-powered insect zapper for a programmer who is fixing bugs right and left (or better yet, not having buggy code in the first place)—or just general fun (in the software world, Nerf toys are always popular). Rewards don't have to be expensive, and fun is always welcome even in a tough environment. (Wondering why I keep talking about making things fun? Current research says that it takes over 400 repetitions to create a synapse in the brain generally—but only about 12 repetitions when taught through play.)[2]

Project managers don't typically have much control over rewards involving **money**, but we can recommend bonuses, awards, or raises based on how well someone is doing. Be aware, though, that the value of the motivation is pretty short-lived. According to research, the effects of even a large raise fade out after four years.[3] When I worked at IBM, I was told that the satisfaction from a raise typically lasted two to four paychecks. Armed with that data, you can feel a bit better if you don't have control over financial rewards.

Some people thrive on **challenge**. They like bleeding-edge technology, seemingly impossible tasks, and anything that others may be afraid to take on. Help these folks out. Assuming your team member is up to the challenge, give those kinds of tasks to her. Don't risk your project, of course, and have a contingency plan in hand, but let her loose on the challenge. If your project doesn't have enough challenge, or if it's mission critical and you need to be really cautious about handing out challenging work, look around for other kinds of challenges. You might be able to loan your team member out part-time to a different team, get her involved in some kind of skunkworks, or set her onto some research that will help your project (or another project in the company) in the future. When you do anything to help satisfy a need for challenge, be sure you spell out the parameters. You don't want your star player to be consumed with something that is a sideline to the main work.

True Story *One organization I worked with had outsourced much of its application development for years. The organization had one department of programmers, which had pretty much faded away due to attrition but had found a need to bring in new programmers to work on the operations side of the application development. A new application was being created with brand-spanking-new technology. Development was scheduled to be outsourced, but this organization's programmers wanted in. They wanted the challenge of new technology. Their management made them a deal: they could run with the project, supplemented by an outsourced team, and own the application when it was done, but they had to commit a certain number of hours a week to the project. That meant that when things got busy on the operations side of their jobs they still had to manage to spend the committed number of hours on this new project in order to complete it on schedule. Not a single programmer hesitated to make that commitment. Things did get busy, including emergency situations on the operations side, but every programmer kept his or her commitment, and the project came in on time, with the programmers reenergized and highly motivated clear through the end of the project.*

You've probably noticed that some of your team members are pretty **competitive**. With any luck, more than one person on the team likes competition. If that's the case, you can generate some friendly competition among the team members with an appropriate reward (something as small as a Starbucks card can work). Who can finish tasks first, who has the fewest defects, whose work gets accepted first, etc. Almost anything on a project can be used to spur competition. The more you can manage the competition, the less risk you run of losing the friendly part of it and losing the cooperation essential to getting projects out the door. If you have only one person on your team who likes competition, you'll need to focus that person on outperforming herself or peers in another group or in another company.

True Story *I was running an incredibly complex software project. It took up an entire division, and as we got close to the release date the number of bugs was piling up. This isn't really unusual in a software project, especially one run in a Waterfall (sequential) process, but we'd used up a lot of contingency time and had a lot of bugs to fix. It was time for a "bugfest." Bugfests aren't that uncommon on software projects; they're a period of time totally dedicated to fixing known defects in the code. Generally programmers aren't too fond of bugfests. Bugfests are boring, bugs can be hard to track down, the programmers are not learning anything new—overall, it's pretty unmotivating. In sheer desperation, I went to my favorite party catalog and bought a bunch of plastic bugs. When I kicked off the bugfest, I announced that each engineer would get a plastic bug for every bug fixed (and verified). QA engineers got one for each bug they verified. (If the bug turned out not to be fixed correctly, both the development engineer and the QA engineer had to give back a bug.) The results were amazing. Everyone wanted to have the most of those little plastic bugs. They were pinned to cube walls, covering keyboards, you name it. I ended up keeping track so we'd have a scorecard. Since that time, I've had bugfests with things like Gummi bugs, and I've given out prizes for the most bugs fixed. (Clearly, everyone on this team was competitive—not surprising, as they were some of the best software engineers in Silicon Valley.)*

Learning something new gives some people great satisfaction. The things they're learning only need to be new to the person, not necessarily bleeding-edge challenges. It's tempting to assign every task to the person who can perform the task absolutely best, but you lose the ability to back up your superstars, and you lose the opportunity for other team members to learn new skills if you never let a person less experienced in an area handle a task. That doesn't mean that everyone should be working on new things all the time, but let those motivated by learning have the chance to learn by doing at least occasionally.

You're likely to run into a few team members who like to **teach**. The problem is that sometimes these folks teach even if the people they're talking with already know the material. This behavior can lead to some irritated team members who feel their time is being wasted (or are offended that someone might think they need to be taught everything). To avoid this problem, find ways to incorporate some kind of teaching into the teaching-motivated team members' responsibilities. Have them mentor new or less experienced team members; set them to research some new tool, process, or technology and bring it back to present to the team; or loan them to another team (briefly or for a few hours a week) to pass on knowledge. These activities will benefit your project by motivating your teachers (and sparing those being taught what they already know) and will benefit your organization by sharing knowledge.

Project managers don't always have the ability to provide much **time off**, but we do have a few tricks available to us. Be sure to build enough contingency into your plans so your team members aren't forced to give up vacation plans to deal with emergencies. Tell someone they've done a good job and should leave a little early on Friday. Ask about vacations and time off when you make your schedules so your team knows you're trying to get them the time they need. If you're not directly managing the team members, let their managers know when they're on the verge of burnout and need a break, and be sure to let their managers know when they're running ahead a little and could use a day off.

Finally, the biggest motivator is always **trust**. Trust people to do the right thing (at least the first time). Give them some space until such time as they show you that space isn't wise. Trust right at the start of your project; don't endanger the project by giving people you're not familiar with too much leeway, but don't micromanage or stand over people unless they've shown you that's what you have to do to get them back on track. (Trust doesn't mean you don't ask questions; if people can't answer reasonable questions about schedule, work progress, etc., there's probably a problem.)

EVERYONE IS GOOD AT SOMETHING

Not only is everyone good at something, but most people like to do the things they're good at. (But not always. People are complicated, so do your research—never assume.) The things they're best at aren't always easy fits for your team or project, but there's usually some application of that something, even a small one, that will help the team out. If there's nowhere in the project to really show it off, see if you can work it into a celebration or team-building event. Most people are motivated by being able to show that they're good at something, especially something they love doing.

The first challenge you face is figuring out what the something is that people are good at. If it's associated directly with work, like coding in a particular language or designing landscapes, the information is probably readily available to you based on their past performance in the company. When it's not directly related, you may need to dig a bit. Those questions I noted that help uncover motivations can also help uncover what people are good at. Finally, never underestimate the power of observation. Really pay attention to what the people on your team are doing and what others on the team respond to. It's passive and seems easy, but with all the juggling we do and all the things on our minds, it takes a few minutes to calm ourselves and just look and listen.

True Story *At one start-up, I ran the technical teams (engineering, QA, Operations, Tech pubs, Support, etc.). We were coming up to an important release, and everyone had worked really hard on it. Everyone had their own personal contributions. As in every department, and especially in start-ups, every person was important in getting the product out the door (and getting us more funding!). We had a party, of course, but I wanted to do something special. A family member of one of my managers did graphic design. She and I came up with what every person in the company (admittedly a small number) did well and had a drawing made of each person doing what they were good at. It wasn't as easy as "this person water-skis." It was more along the lines of "calm under pressure" and "solves even the gnarliest code issues." I got inexpensive frames for them, and we gave them out at the launch. What I remember most is that I got one too. It was a big surprise, but I still have it 20 years later. It's a drawing of me in Renaissance Irish garb (I'm of Irish heritage) raising a staff, and the caption is "Kim the Snake Charmer," a reference to getting people to do things that they really don't want to and to play nicely together even under extreme pressure. Twenty years, and still motivating. That's what we're trying to achieve.*

INDIVIDUAL GOALS

Everyone has goals. Sometimes they're written down in yearly plans, sometimes they're long term, sometimes they're just in people's heads. Goals often feed motivation and vice versa, so it's good to work to uncover individual goals. Sometimes you can work these into your project plan so people can work toward or even achieve goals within the work of the project. Goals are usually a lot easier to uncover than motivation—people know their own goals even if they're not actively working on them. I usually just ask people what their short-term and long-term goals are and whether they see anything immediate in the project that might help them work toward those goals, and then I look for places I can help out while still keeping the project on track.

WORKING WITH VOLUNTEERS

Some of us actually work for nonprofits and manage projects partly or fully staffed with volunteers. Some of us work with our favorite community organizations and always end up organizing events and other efforts. Even if you never run projects staffed with volunteers, you will probably at some time have subject matter experts, advisors, or people from other teams helping you out on a project. In all these cases you're working with someone who is not depending on a project's success or their contribution to it to earn their living.

Volunteers are another species entirely than paid staff and you'll need to modify your approach to keep your volunteers happy and, well, volunteering.

People volunteer for many reasons, and you don't have a lot of time to uncover their motivation before you lose them altogether. The best way is just to ask, either "Why are you here?" or "What would you like to work on?" Don't just randomly fill out a work list, or you'll miss the chance to establish a solid ongoing relationship with your volunteers. Having a volunteer walk off can throw a monkey wrench into the works both in long-term efforts (for example, putting on a play and having someone doing costuming walk off might leave your actors in the lurch) and single events (imagine what chaos would ensue if your registration person for a walk-a-thon abruptly leaves in the middle of the event). You can ask what the volunteer does for a living. That doesn't mean he is looking to do the same thing as a volunteer, but usually he'll let you know one way or the other. If he doesn't, just ask the follow-up question of whether he wants to use that professional skill on the volunteer project. If you have someone who loves art and wants to be creative, you can put her on sets or have her figure out a new way to run a process that isn't working. If you have someone who likes to be in charge, have him direct whatever traffic is involved in the effort.

People don't always walk out when their motivations aren't being met. It gets worse than that. Imagine this situation: You've called for volunteers at your child's school to get new library computers up and running. You have your experts, but you need people who can follow instructions to implement the directions. You don't have a lot of time to do this, because the system can't be down for too long without impacting teachers and students. One parent has volunteered because she wants to observe her child in the classroom environment, but you don't know that. Instead of following the directions, she ends up heading to her child's classroom on one pretext or another. In this case, you've lost a volunteer midstream and are impacting everyone else on this short-term project. Because you didn't prescreen for motivation ahead of time (when you could have suggested she volunteer for some classroom activity instead of yours since she probably thought she'd be doing the work from the classroom), you've impacted the team and possibly the timeline.

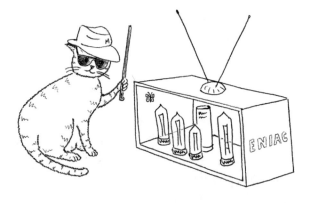

GET OUT YOUR SECRET AGENT GLASSES

Why Aren't They Listening?!

Sometimes you have to do some reconnaissance to understand how to approach people, how best to communicate with them, and how to get them to respond. Everyone is busy, everyone is deluged with information these days. The trick is to figure out how to get yourself at the top of people's lists. A little undercover work can go a long way.

True Story *A project manager I worked with was having a rough week. There were problems with one of her applications and the programmer was working hard to find a way to fix them. She told me how frustrated she was with the programmer because she was sending him emails asking for status and information, and he sent one-word email responses. Because she was trying to juggle so many things that particular day she continued to send emails instead of using other communication—and continued to get single-word replies that didn't explain enough for her to tell management what was happening. I suggested that the project manager walk over to the programmer's desk, even though she was feeling underwater, and talk to him. She called me back later to tell me that he was very forthcoming with her when she was in his office, and she understood all the details after talking with him.*

So why the big difference in the programmer's responses to email and face-to-face communication? The answer to this puzzle is easy—the programmer didn't communicate well in email. He wasn't being difficult or obtuse, he just wasn't comfortable with long emails. How did I know that? Truthfully, I didn't. What I did know is that learning styles have a lot to do with how people communicate, and I thought a change in approach might work. I use learning styles (which translate to working and communication styles) constantly in my project management work.

The five learning styles I work with are these:

- Visual
- Reading
- Auditory
- Tactile
- Kinetic

Some other peripheral styles have turned up, but they tend to be less useful in project management, so I focus on the main styles.

LEARNING (WORKING) STYLES

Learning styles are the result of research performed in the 1970s. The initial research showed that everyone takes in information *best* in one of a few ways. Everyone can learn in all the available modes, but one or sometimes two ways are easiest and best for that person. The initial research addressed three learning styles.

For a long time learning styles were primarily used in elementary school education (if you ever used SRA Reading, you've seen one application of the research).

In the first years of the twenty-first century, neuroscience finally caught up with the initial behavioral research. An explosion of physiological information was suddenly available to support the theory, and learning styles started to be applied in all sorts of interesting places. (You may know that the jury is still out after all these years on whether children actually learn any faster or test any better using their preferred styles. That's true, but it doesn't affect the application of the styles for our purposes.) The main advantage I've found in observing and applying learning styles to individual interactions is that approaching a busy person in her preferred style gets me a higher ranking in her attention and processing list—and that's invaluable.

Visual

Visual learning is exactly what you'd expect—visual learners learn best when information is highly graphic.

For years, I've put a small picture or graphic on every slide in every presentation. Until I understood more about learning styles I didn't know why it seemed to help people focus on the presentation, I just knew that it worked. Now I know that visual learners immediately look at the graphic to understand the theme of the slide.

Most of the C-level executives I've worked with seem to be visual learners or to at least have visual as one of their preferred modes. (Whether visual learners are more inclined to be C-level execs or whether C-level execs learn to look for graphics out of necessity to process the huge flow of information coming at them isn't clear to me. In any case it's a really good idea to have graphics for executive presentations.)

Charts and graphs are the right place to start for visual learners. Color and other markers (bold, italic, underlining, outline form) will help your visual learners prioritize information.

Rules for Engaging Visual Learners:

- Summarize information whenever possible and provide the details as backup. (Not only will this help keep your visual learners engaged and on the same page as the rest of the team, it's just good project management practice.)

- Use charts wherever possible to provide an overview of numerical information.
- Bring pictures when you can. Visual learners like screen sharing, for example. Even a comic to start a meeting will help engage visual learners.
- Put some kind of graphic (it can be small—I use a small square on the upper right of the page title) on every page possible for presentations.
- Provide written information in outline form, using bold and color (be careful with red and green in case you have color-blind visual learners), to make important information easily visible.

If you look immediately to the graphics or pictures in a presentation or report, you're probably a visual learner. Likewise, if you go online and look for video reports instead of printed reports, you're probably a visual learner.

Reading

The reading learning style is a relatively new addition. The original list of learning styles included text in the Visual style; Reading (sometimes called Reading/Writing) was determined later to be a separate, if related, learning style.

Written words are best for reading learners. Reading learners will usually want to see the actual data or detail behind charts and graphs. Summary information is fine for reading learners, but they will always be looking for the details.

Reading learners typically respond well to email. They're the ones who actually read your minutes and status reports and reply quickly to emails you send. They may not answer phone calls right away, and they may ask you to send a written summary of information you just discussed.

Rules for Engaging Reading Learners:

- Provide at least some text when you can.
- Add the data to any charts and graphs (this is low-hanging fruit; it's just a chart option).
- Follow up any information provided via meetings or presentations with a written version.

If you read through every item on every page of a presentation, if you get annoyed when presentation slides are shown one line at a time, or if you turn off the video on your internet news reports, you're probably a reading learner.

Auditory

Auditory learning is, if you'll excuse the expression, exactly what it sounds like. Auditory learners process information best when they can hear it.

Written minutes, agendas, and other information can be more difficult for auditory learners to process if they are not read aloud at some point. (Auditory learners *can* process written information, of course, but will procrastinate in favor of any kind of auditory information.)

Auditory learners typically love phone calls. They'll pick up on the first ring when you call but may never answer (and maybe not even read) your emails.

Rules for Engaging Auditory Learners:

- Read the agenda out loud at the beginning of every meeting.
- Speak to bullet points on slides (no, don't read off the page; that's just annoying). As a corollary, never stand back and say, "Well, you can read this for yourself." Your auditory learners won't actually do the reading.

49

- Before you end a meeting, summarize the decisions and action items out loud.
- Follow up emails or printed deliveries that need a response with a phone call.

If you love podcasts, if you pick up the phone before you bother to look at emails, if you listen to speakers without really looking at the presentation, you're probably an auditory learner.

Tactile

Tactile learners absorb information best when it can be touched.

Tactile learners take notes, even when handouts are provided. It's a way of touching the information; they may never read their notes after writing them. (You could provide an entire transcript and tactile learners would still take notes). Note cards, sticky notes, things that can be touched will help tactile learners. Tactile learners like to write on a whiteboard (or blackboard or easel pad).

Rules for Engaging Tactile Learners:

- Provide printed versions of online information if it's not available before its use (for example, new documents for a meeting that you didn't send out ahead of time. Print a few copies out even if you're going over it in detail visually or in discussion). You'll be able to tell which are the tactile learners in your regular meetings; they'll print out copies themselves and bring them to the meetings.
- Always provide a few printed copies of the agenda and any information sent ahead of time for any meetings that aren't recurring. We don't want to kill a lot of trees, so a few copies will do unless you have an entire team of tactile learners.
- Encourage writing on any available whiteboard or similar surface.

If your monitor or workspace is full of sticky notes, if you carry a notebook everywhere even when you have electronic tools available, if your to-do list is always on paper, or if you love flash cards and note cards, you're probably a tactile learner.

Kinetic

The final learning style is kinetic. Kinetic learners need to move either the information or themselves to process most easily. Kinetic is a relatively new classification (not part of the original study), and is closely related to tactile. (Some surveys are putting them together at this point, but there are subtle differences.)

Kinetic learners also take notes or sometimes just doodle in the margins. These are the people who are always tapping a pen or a foot, shuffling notes, or walking around. They're not doing it to annoy you; they just need to have some movement to help process information.

As a side note, as a kinetic learner myself, I've found (via injudicious but fortuitous screen sharing at a time when games came with operating systems) that many kinetic learners play solitaire during meetings to help focus. (There are a million solitaire games for phones, and you can bet most kinetic users have at least one version on theirs.) The game uses little mindshare but provides motion. If you have someone who looks like he's checking email during a meeting but is keeping up and contributing, he's probably a kinetic learner providing himself some motion. Kinetic learners also like using whiteboards and are more engaged when others are using them.

Rules for Engaging Kinetic Learners:

- As with tactile learners, provide printouts where appropriate.
- If it's not too distracting, let people walk around during your meetings (have true stand-up meetings).

- If someone is looking at their electronic device but clearly engaged in the meeting or conversation, don't comment on it.
- Encourage whiteboard (or similar surface) use.

There's a difference I've noticed between tactile learners at a whiteboard and kinetic learners at a whiteboard. Tactile learners write on the board and put the marker down. Kinetic learners write on the board and then play with the marker.

If you do the solitaire thing, if you take notes, if you doodle without worrying about words, if you can concentrate better if you're up and moving, you're probably a kinetic learner.

How Do I Tell?

The big question—how do you know what person prefers what learning style?

There are online tests—just google "learning style test" and you'll get a list of free tools. (If you want people to take a test, be prepared to take it yourself and share the results.)

The easiest way, though, is through observation (use those secret agent glasses). Notice how each person responds to email, phone calls, etc.; notice how each person behaves in meetings (even in one-on-one meetings). Need some clues?

Visual Learner Clues

If you lose someone's attention when you're presenting a lot of detailed written information, he's probably visual.

If someone sits up and takes notice when you show a graph or chart, she's probably visual.

If someone brings up points you've made in writing using bold font or a bright color, he's probably visual.

If someone says, "I see," when she understands, she's probably visual.

If someone prints the map picture but not the directions when he looks up a destination on MapQuest, he's probably visual.

Reading Learner Clues

If someone responds quickly and predictably to email, she's probably reading.

If someone consistently wants to see the details behind a chart or summary, he's probably reading.

If someone usually asks you to send the info in email when you've just discussed it, she's probably reading.

If someone prints the directions but not the map picture when he looks up a destination on MapQuest, he's probably reading.

Auditory Learner Clues

If someone picks up the phone every time you call but never seems to respond to emails, she's probably auditory.

If someone doesn't look at the materials you bring to a meeting but focuses on the speaker, he's probably auditory.

Tactile Learner Clues

If someone has sticky notes around her working space (*lots* of sticky notes), she's probably tactile.

If someone prints out the agenda and brings it to the meeting, he's probably tactile.

If someone is always taking notes but sits quietly, she's probably tactile.

Kinetic Learner Clues

If someone seems to have trouble keeping still, he's probably kinetic.

If someone likes to wander around as she speaks, she's probably kinetic.

If someone always talks with his hands, he's probably kinetic.

If someone always wants to go to the whiteboard (and keeps the marker in hand), she's probably kinetic.

More than One Style

Most people take in information most easily in one or two of the learning styles. I have only worked with one person who felt he could learn equally from all modes, and I definitely believe him (he's a sponge), but he's the exception. Don't be put off if you see signs of more than one favorite learning style in a person; it only makes communication easier.

So What Do I Do with This Learning Styles Stuff?

The first step is to figure out how the people on your team absorb information most easily. One of the keys to managing a project is communication, and that applies to people being able to process your information as well as to your sending communication effectively. Once you know each person's learning style you can approach team members in whatever way is easiest for each. This isn't as hard as it sounds.

Pick up the phone instead of emailing auditory learners, or if you've sent a group email, do a quick follow-up on the phone or in person.

Send notes and minutes in outline form, using bold and color to help your visual learners.

Be sure to include graphics in your presentations.

Start with a summary and provide details as backup.

Send presentation materials and agendas ahead of time.

Bring a few printed copies of meeting materials to any meeting.

It's mostly just a matter of paying attention, formatting written materials and presentations in a way that can be used by all the learning styles, and checking to be sure that everyone is on the same page.

TRY IT

Here's a meeting in progress. How do you read the room?

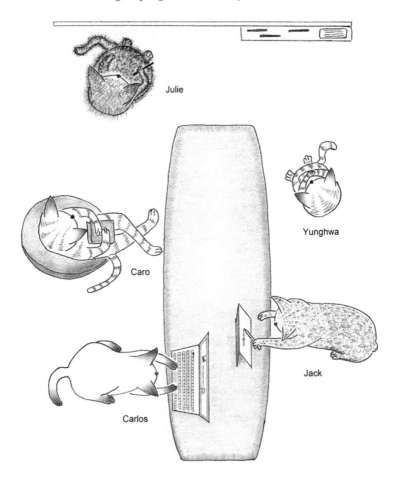

- Julie is standing at the whiteboard, marker in hand, having presented information.
- Jack is furiously taking notes.
- Caro is sitting back listening to Julie.

- Yunghwa is studying the diagram Julie has drawn on the whiteboard.
- Carlos seems to be reading his email but has a comment on what Julie just wrote.

What style is each person in the room?

ANSWER

- Julie is kinetic; she's at the whiteboard and the marker is in her hand.
- Jack is tactile, taking notes.
- Caro is auditory, listening without looking at the board.
- Yunghwa is visual, looking first to the diagram on the board.
- Carlos is kinetic; he's probably playing a game but is fully engaged.

TIPS FOR TRIUMPHANT PRESENTATIONS

Want to make your presentation memorable (in a good way, of course)? Social intelligence, particularly attention to learning styles, can get you there.

Many of us make presentations to audiences of people we don't know or at least don't work with all the time. It's convenient to build the presentation around the people in the audience who you know or the decision makers in the audience; unfortunately, taking this shortcut can alienate the people whose learning style isn't addressed by your presentation style.

It's pretty easy to make presentations work for everyone in the room, even when you don't know them. (I've bundled all the learning style details for presentations I've already given you plus a few extras so you can grab it when you're creating a presentation.)

First, **have some visuals**. If your primary audience is someone who doesn't like visuals, or at least doesn't pay attention to them, and you know that coming with a slide deck is going to annoy the decision maker, you'll need to go to paper. Create your slide deck and print copies of it. If you're not up against this particular problem, print out a few copies but make the slide deck your go-to presentation.

You may want to use my own device of having some kind of picture or graphic on every page. That will help focus the visual learners (and it's a nice break from lots of words on slides).

Start with a summary, and have the details as backup. This should be done for every proposal, recommendation, and conclusion. Pages and pages of data charts might be nice for a few people, and it's good to have them as backup, but don't go into the details unless it's clear your audience is interested. (It's even okay to ask if anyone wants more detail, and let them know you have it. Offer to send it in email if only one or two people want the detail, assuming those one or two people don't include the decision maker.)

Starting with a summary should satisfy the visual learners as well as those more detail oriented among your audience. Avoid the two traps associated with this: First, don't skip putting the detail together. It's always good to have it, it can keep you from making mistakes in the summary, and it makes you more knowledgeable in general, even if it's more work. Second, don't walk through all the detail just because you have it. Unless your audience really wants to see the detail, they'll lose interest in your presentation altogether.

Okay, now we've satisfied the visual learners and, to some extent, the reading learners. Be sure you **have words on your slides, but don't have paragraphs**. The words on the slides should be a small subset of the words you'll be saying to go with the written material or slides. This will satisfy the reading learners without alienating other learning styles.

Don't ever say, "Well, you can read it here on the slide." Your auditory learners don't *want* to read it, and in most cases they won't bother.

Be sure to **cover all the important points verbally.** This will help keep the auditory learners on track.

Bring a few printed copies of your presentation. If the presentation is too large, bring a few printed copies of the most important pages of it. This will help the kinetic and tactile users stay engaged.

Move around. This will help the kinetic learners, as well as help focus everyone on you. This means you don't get to sit at the head of the table and read the slides or agenda to the room. You're moving, being engaged, and engaging the people around you.

Finally, don't be afraid to illustrate a point, run problem-solving, or have an exercise involving **writing on a whiteboard or flipchart**.

It sounds like a lot, but you can easily combine all these tips into a single presentation without a lot of additional work. It's just a matter of organization, focus, and remembering the different learning styles and what works for them.

AN EXAMPLE OF PRESENTATION FORMATTING STRATEGY

I present at conferences and in companies, and I teach workshops. I get uniformly good reviews, and I know part of the reason for those reviews is that I organize for all the learning styles. In a typical workshop or presentation, I'll have all of these, and I move around a lot when I'm presenting (for the kinetic folks, including me):

- **Slides**
- **Words** on the slides (but not too many)
- **Detail** for backup
- A **picture, chart, or graphic** on every slide
- **Exercises** so people can try things out themselves (not always appropriate; depends on the presentation)
- **Group exercises** so those people who like to connect and exchange information get a chance (not always appropriate)
- A **video** that's pertinent
- Something **fun** or funny (unless I'm reporting an issue or its resolution)
- A chance for the audience to **contribute**
- A chance to ask **questions**. I rarely save questions until the end because people forget what they wanted to ask

SURVEYS, PROFILES, AND PERSONALITY TESTS

There is no shortage of tests that profile people into categories of some sort. The most well-known of these is the Myers-Briggs personality inventory, but there are many more.

Tests and categorizations can certainly be useful. They give people insight into their own behavior and preferences and can provide the same kind of insight to team members. They can be fun to take and compare, and many teams do just that. It can even be a team-building exercise. I've taken quite a few of them, from Myers-Briggs via the Keirsey sorter (a much shorter version of the Myers-Briggs test that you can sometimes find for free online) to tests and surveys that help with rewards and recognition for individuals.

The caution with these tests is that they sometimes lead to pigeonholing people, giving them a label and addressing them as a label instead of as a complex personality. Be aware also that for many of the tests and many people the categorization can change as circumstances change, even by the hour.

True Story *I took a version of the Myers-Briggs test using the Keirsey sorter in a master's course on creativity in groups. One of my team members saw my results sitting on the printer and asked about it. Word spread quickly, and by the end of the day everyone on my team and quite a few other people had taken the test. It was a great conversation starter and definitely helped with understanding the reactions of others in the group; however, some people took it again the next day and had slightly different results. Most who retook it were just curious, but some were trying to see if they could influence the results. It was a great follow-up to the previous hallway discussions on "What are you?" and kept the pigeonholing to a minimum.*

GET 'EM COMING AND GOING

Meetings People Show Up for and Minutes People Read

We're project managers. That means that we're the queens and kings of meetings. We get people together, we get them on the same page, we work things out. Love 'em or hate 'em, we have to have meetings.

Even though you get lots of information now because people on your team trust you and you're able to get information out to them one-on-one in their preferred communication style, they still hate meetings. *You* know that everyone needs to get together to hear things at the same time and have a discussion with all the right people in the room, but sometimes even you would like to avoid your own meetings. People come in late, don't pay attention, don't participate, or even hijack the meeting to talk about their favorite topic. Action items are never done and keep carrying over to the next meeting. And no one even looks at the minutes, even people who weren't in the meeting. Does any of this sound familiar?

But you can have meetings that are productive, with everyone showing up on time, action items done, and minutes (at least the most important parts of them) read if you follow a few simple rules. Some of these rules are based on the communication styles we talked about earlier, some have to do with managing both the people in the meeting and the time allotted, and some of them are really just simple formatting and timing rules. We have to have meetings and minutes, but they don't have to be painful.

One other tip before we get to the heart of the subject: I *always* take and send my own minutes. Why? For the simple reason that she who sends the minutes controls the reality of the meeting. In most situations we don't provide transcripts of meetings; the minutes only cover the most important points discussed. I want people to remember those topics and decisions that *I* consider important. It's my project (and my meeting), after all.

MEETINGS THAT CLICK

The first question to ask when you're getting ready to schedule a meeting is, Do I really need a meeting? There's a reason the T-shirt with "I survived another meeting that should have been an email" on it is so popular. Think it through and be sure a meeting is the best vehicle for whatever you're trying to accomplish. A corollary to this is that if you have a meeting scheduled and you find you don't need it—the issue has been resolved, it's a regular meeting with no agenda items this week, information that's needed isn't available yet—cancel it. Seriously. People will celebrate that extra hour to get things done. (Don't you? One of the most basic keys to working well with people is to put yourself in their place. How would *you* feel or react in the situation if your roles were reversed?)

Most people see meetings as something to get through so they can do their actual work and often skip meetings or spend most of the meeting doing other work. So how do you make your meetings the ones people show up for, pay attention in, and believe are useful? This is a great place to apply both social intelligence and common sense.

The Agenda: They're often last-minute (when we create them at all), but with a little thought, your meeting agenda can turn into a very useful tool instead of one more task to check off the list. Your agenda should be out the day before your meeting, even if it's a weekly meeting with a fixed agenda. Remind everyone of the meeting location and/or call-in information so they don't have to search for it. Include the topics in the order you'll address them, and the first item should be "review agenda." Just as importantly, include all the current action items in the agenda—don't forget any that have been closed since the last meeting. In my experience, 90 percent of action items are completed between the time I send them in my agenda and the meeting. People often forget they even have action items, and no one likes to see their name on a late action item.

Creating an agenda not only ensures that people prepare for your meeting; it also helps you think through what you need to discuss, decide if you still need the meeting, and keep the meeting on track when you're in the middle of it.

True Story *I worked with one company that set up a daily meeting to discuss requirements (the market was in flux and product requirements changed pretty regularly). This meeting never had any agenda. It would go on, literally, for hours. Every single day. No one knew how to prepare for it, no one knew what decisions were needed, and worst of all no one knew when it was done. Everyone invited worked hard to get out of it, and the meeting usually ended up being just two guys sitting there, going around and around on the same material. It was a total waste of time, and people avoided going near that room while the meeting was starting or going on for fear they'd be called in. An agenda would have made short work of it, especially since it was running every day.*

If the meeting has people showing up in person (not just on phone or videoconference), *bring a printed copy or two* of the agenda and any materials you'll be discussing in the meeting. I know, we're all trying to go paperless, but this is where we lose some of the people who need to touch the information. The tactile and kinetic learners in the meeting will appreciate it, and if they haven't printed their own before the meeting, they'll grab a copy as soon as they see it.

Once you've set the agenda, **decide who needs to be in the meeting**. If people can get by with just knowing the results, or if you're putting someone on the agenda "just in case" or because you know she's interested, make her optional. Be sure you have everyone you really need to achieve the goals of the meeting on the required list, but give people confidence that they're coming to a meeting because they're needed.

Start and end on time. Unless the person who is the reason for the meeting hasn't shown up yet (the decision maker or your CEO, for example), *start the meeting on time*. If you wait for everyone to straggle in, people will start coming later (and later and later) because they'd rather be checking their email than waiting in a meeting room for latecomers. If you always start on time, people will start showing up on time. (If you know that some or all of the people in your meeting will be running from another meeting to get to yours, just schedule the meeting to start five minutes later. I know it will offend the sensibilities of those who like all things to be even, but you *can* officially start a meeting at 10:05 instead of 10:00.) Starting on time not only gets people into your meeting but also shows respect for everyone's time.

Sometimes we don't get through the whole agenda, but it's still important to **end meetings on time**. If *everyone* in the meeting says they're free to continue, go ahead. If not, either finish up in email or schedule a follow-on meeting. If people need to be somewhere else, they won't pay attention or contribute; they'll be fuming and looking for an escape. If some people can't stay and you continue the meeting, you're pretty much announcing that those people who are leaving aren't important. The way you structure your agenda can make a big difference in how this plays out. Anything important and quick should be at the beginning of your agenda so that those items are addressed. Anything not critical that could wait until the next meeting should be at the end of your agenda. Anything important and likely to run long should be after the quick or important items so you have time to discuss them. (If you're having a regular meeting like a status meeting and you know one item will suck up all the time and then some, schedule it in a different meeting and invite only the people you need for that topic instead of derailing your status meeting.) Again, show respect and use common sense.

Always **start with summary information**. If everyone is comfortable with the summary and there are no questions on the details, don't belabor a topic. Certainly, go into details when there's disagreement, misunderstanding, or when it's a new topic and people don't have full information, but don't waste everyone's time if they're clear on the details.

Cater to the styles of the meeting attendees. People will be more involved and will remember more about the content of the meeting.

The visual learners will get bored if there's nothing to look at. Whenever possible, *have a picture, a chart, something colorful* to help them engage. One great way to start a meeting is with some kind of cartoon. You'll want to keep an eye out for these and collect them to show at the beginning of your meetings. A cartoon or drawing has the advantage of starting a meeting in an upbeat way, and if you only show it for a minute or two you'll also be encouraging the habitual latecomers to show up on time.

If you're in a meeting room with a whiteboard (or the equivalent), encourage people to use it. This will help the kinetic and tactile learners participate. (If you're comfortable using the whiteboard, get the party started yourself by writing on it.) If you're teleconferencing, use a whiteboard or sharing tool and encourage people to share documents they're referring to or to use the tool as a virtual whiteboard.

The kinetic learners will need to walk around or do something with movement. If the meeting is long, most people will benefit from a quick stretch and you'll get better results faster. *Be sure to let people know it's okay to move around a bit during the meeting (as long as it's not disruptive).*

If this isn't a regularly repeating meeting, *bring a few hard copies* of the agenda and other materials (even though you sent them out in advance). This will help the tactile users engage.

We spend lots of meeting time on the phone or VOIP. People can easily get lost when you can't see them. **Videoconference whenever possible**. People pay more attention, and it feels more like a team than listening to a bunch of disembodied voices. When you don't have video available you'll need to do a few other things to keep people engaged. First, if someone says something quietly or there's noise on the line, either repeat it yourself or ask the person to repeat it. For some reason, even though most people are anxious to be sure they've been heard and happy to repeat themselves, most people are also reluctant to ask someone else to repeat what they said. If a group is in another location, have some kind of Instant Messaging going during the call with someone in the group you're comfortable with. That person can alert you when people are looking lost, not understanding, not hearing the conversation well, having translation problems—the kinds of things you'd pick up on if you were in the room. That person can also tell you who all is in the room with them, which will help with the minutes.

Start with a roll call so everyone knows who all is on the call. (Pay attention; you'll need this information when you put together the minutes. This is one place where your contacts in the other locations can help—you may not catch everyone's name as they say it, but you can have your contacts email or IM the info to you.)

If you're working across time zones and some members of the team will be working very early or very late to attend the call, consider rotating the time. It's a little more difficult to manage the schedule, but it will help everyone feel like an equal member of the team. (It will also provide a small thing in common for everyone on the team—complaining about a meeting "at this hour.") If the scheduling gets too complicated, consider scheduling on a monthly or quarterly basis (so you have it, say, early on the West Coast of the United States for a month and then late in the evening in Europe the next month).

MEETINGS WITH VOLUNTEERS

All the important bits about meetings in your business life apply to meetings with volunteers, but meetings with volunteers have some special, um, considerations.

First, you'll need to have a central location that's generally convenient, or people won't come. If it's out of the way, you'll need to provide good descriptions of the place and directions for getting there. It's a lot easier to opt out of a meeting if it's dark and you can't find the place than it is if it's at a school or community center. Make your contact information available, and tell people to let you know if they're not going to make it so you're not waiting for them. Don't make that contact so difficult that they don't tell you when they're going to skip a meeting (in other words, don't be disapproving when they call); it's better to know they're not coming. If someone misses a lot of the meetings, it's a sign. Either they're not that interested, you've assigned them something that doesn't suit them, or they're just too busy even though they want to do it. You may want to put them in a noncritical role so they don't impact the project and to make it less stressful for the volunteer.

People tend to straggle into volunteer meetings. Everyone is coming from somewhere different and has different demands on their time. Accommodate this to some extent—maybe make the first 10 minutes social time. Be sure all the key players have arrived before you cover essential topics.

In business meetings we're pretty used to covering topics, making decisions, and moving on. When you work with volunteers you'll find that everyone doesn't work that way. Some people arrive at conclusions by meandering and discussing. You'll have to figure out if there's a group methodology that works. If there is, structure your meeting for discussion. If there isn't, you'll need to do some thinking about the meeting structure so you don't lose people.

End the official part of the meeting on time, but allow time for people to hang out and talk things over or socialize.

When you have larger meetings—calls for volunteers, informational meetings, etc.—take your time to plan the meeting the whole way through.

Think about food (see Step 9), because people get cranky when their blood sugar gets low, and they're a lot more willing to show that grumpiness in a volunteer situation.

Address all the learning types since you're only going to have one chance to do it to keep people in the meeting. If you'll be having more than one of the extended meetings, you want people to remember how fun it was and to tell that to those who didn't come.

This leads us to another important tip: the extended meetings should be as fun as you can make them (depending on the subject matter). Make some jokes, play some music, present things in a fun way with comics or skits. You're working with a lot of different people, typically at the end of a workday or a work week, and you need to keep things moving and interesting.

Practice what you're going to say so that you're confident and your potential volunteers feel like they're going to participate in a winning effort.

True Story *I volunteered to run Grad Night at my daughter's high school her senior year. It was a big event with a secret theme, held on the grounds of the school. Decorations alone took six months, and there were games, picture walls, a story board and photograph room, a casino, a live band, magicians, a salon, temporary tattoos, a photo booth, and even masseuses. It took about 3,500 volunteer hours to put on, plus lots of people at the event to run it (it lasted from about 7:00 at night until 7:00 the next morning). I thought, what the heck, I'm a project manager; I run things.*

Not so fast.

I ran into serious problems with the meetings of committee heads. Everyone preferred to have meetings at the members' homes (since arranging evening times at the school took some effort and could hamper surprises we were planning), but the homes had to be in town and have enough parking and room for a steering committee of about a dozen people. My house was too far away, so I had to arrange meetings at committee members' houses, often having to beg.

This was really my first serious brush with the meandering method of exploration and decision-making, and I didn't want to alienate the people who were working that way. Unfortunately, this completely frustrated the business people on the committee who (like me) were used to running through an agenda and getting on with things. What I finally did was put those businesspeople at the top of the agenda (right after announcements and critical decisions they needed to be part of). I made it clear that they could head out if they wanted after they gave their reports. That meant that I had to catch them up separately on anything they needed to know that came up later in the meeting, but that was much better than having them quit the effort! Once I made this adjustment, things got back into a better place where everyone could contribute in the way they felt most comfortable.

Extended meetings to let the parents of seniors in on what was happening and try to drum up volunteers were a production. I always had food, usually cookies and fruit, and water available. The extended meetings were in a central and well-known location (next to the school). The theme was "The Adventure Continues," so I showed up in an Indiana Jones hat with a whip, and we played the Indiana Jones theme music when we announced it. We put the sign-up tables near each of the doors (mean, I know, but it meant that people couldn't really sneak past) and had lots of information available about what kind of volunteers were needed as well as who to contact. All this worked pretty well—we had enough volunteers and a full house for subsequent meetings.

MINUTES THAT PEOPLE ACTUALLY READ

The first thing is to always, *always*, send minutes of your meetings. If nothing else, they're a record of who was there and what happened. They don't have to be long or complicated, but people should absolutely expect minutes from you after your meetings.

I know, minutes are boring and time consuming. Minutes are often the first thing to go when we get into a time crunch, but they are endlessly useful. Minutes provide a record of decisions made so you don't have to revisit them. Minutes provide information on who was (and wasn't) in any given meeting (that is, who was part of the decision-making process). Minutes are a handy place to remind people of action items. They really can save you a lot of trouble; when everyone knows minutes exist, they rarely argue the outcome of any given meeting.

Not only should you always send minutes (and depending on your team, you can call them notes, which is somewhat less intimidating), you should **get them out within 24 hours** of the meeting. Same-day minutes are ideal because it's sometimes hard to decipher notes the next day.

The first line of your minutes is a **list of attendees**. People always look for their own names, and if you can get them looking at the list to be sure they're on it, there's a good chance they'll read further.

Remember that minutes aren't transcripts. You don't have to have every little detail; in fact, you can use minutes to highlight the information you want people to remember. **Summarize whenever possible.** This doesn't mean you don't provide any detail at all—be sure to have everything your reader will need (and that you'll need to remember later), but make the detail easy to separate from the summary information.

Over the years I've found that an **outline form** is best. No one but the reading learners are going to read through a bunch of paragraphs of text (even the reading learners might not), so outlining using bullet points helps everyone find what they need quickly. This is particularly important for the visual learners. An outline format will also help you find information later if you're searching. Forget about complete sentences in minutes—short and to the point is always best (sorry English majors). Outline form is the easiest way to separate summary from detail; use sub-bullets for the details.

Your minutes don't have to follow the actual flow of the meeting. **Put decisions made up front**—if people stop reading, you want them to have gotten through the decisions that were made. On the assumption that readers are likely to be interrupted before they're done, put the most important information earlier in the minutes.

Use **color**, **bold**, and **italics** to make it easier for the reader to find the important points. (Don't overdo it though, or people will feel like you're not serious.) This is especially important for the visual learners; they'll be looking for visual clues. Do be aware that red-green color blindness is more prevalent than you might think (and people usually don't tell you if they have it), so using red and green as markers might not be as effective as you'd like.

Be sure to include a **table of action items**. They can be at the bottom of minutes because people will, again, be looking for their own names. Note action items that were completed since the last meeting—everyone likes to see a "COMPLETE" beside an action item they've finished. Include assignees and due or promised dates on the action items.

Finally, **always include the text of the minutes in an email**. Many of us send beautiful attachments with the minutes or a link to an intranet site with the minutes, but almost no one opens the attachment or follows the link. Attachments and links are fine but only if you also copy the text into the email. It seems simple enough, but for some reason opening an attachment or clicking a link is a barrier to entry that people don't overcome. (This is another fact of project management life where it's better to just accept it as fact instead of being frustrated about it, à la "If only people would just do their job!")

True Story *At one company some project managers post minutes of meetings on an intranet behind a firewall, never sending the text of the meetings. I attend a lot of meetings at that company, and I can tell you that I almost never read minutes posted this way. Many of the employees of the company work from home regularly, so they're not always behind the firewall, and I expect they also don't bother with the double effort of getting through the firewall and then finding the right page for the notes. In other words, posting behind a firewall is good for reference if a question comes up, but if you want people to actually read minutes, you have to make access easy.*

MINUTES FOR VOLUNTEERS

I've found that volunteers often won't read minutes of meetings (unless they're those people you let leave early so others could meander). Make a full version available, but have a short version: who was there, decisions made, and action items. You will probably need to remind people that they have action items coming up, as volunteers often don't read agendas you send either. It's a little more work, but since you're likely to be tracking action items and deadlines anyway, it's not so hard to follow up with email, text, or voice reminders in enough time for people to react.

STEP 5

FIND YOUR TRIBE

The Personality of a Team

Have you ever noticed that one team member leaving and another joining makes the whole team seem different? That's because every team has its own personality, blending the skills, motivations, worldview, and interactions of the various members. Once you understand what makes your team *members* tick, you need to figure out what makes your *team* run. You can work on team building at the same time that you're establishing relationships with the individual team members.

Start building your team by considering both hard skills and soft skills. Hard skills are pretty easy to spot. They're testable and usually appear on a résumé. When you're interviewing you can ask specific questions to assess someone's level in a hard skill. Think of things like Java programming, carpentry, test creation, technical writing—things that are easy to evaluate. These of course are very important in creating a team. You certainly want team members who are up to the technical task, and we usually try to get the best available for the hard skills we need. (Be careful even with this. If you don't need, say, a senior programmer but you want one just the same, you may end up with a very bored senior programmer who wants to be doing something else and therefore can be disruptive to the team. Get the skill level you need.)

Soft skills are harder to define and assess. They rarely show up on résumés or CVs, and you need to be skilled at behavioral interviewing to get any idea at all of someone's soft skills. These are skills like communicating, presenting, and team building. They seem secondary when you're looking at hard skills, but the soft skills can make or break a team. You have three tasks with respect to soft skills on your team. First, you need to understand what soft skills you need. This is a combination of the project profile and to some extent the soft skills of other members of the team. Your second task is to assess soft skills of candidates or team members. Since we don't always get to staff our own teams, you may need to do a quick assessment of the soft skills of the team members assigned to you. That will help you focus your own work so you can fill in any gaps in soft skills left after the team is staffed. Finally, you need to develop and enhance the soft skills of your team members. You're going to need to do this pretty quickly if you have any significant gaps. If you have the basic soft skills you need, it's more a matter of recognizing potential and pairing people up for learning or getting people some assignments to build experience in the skills you're working to enhance. This isn't really much different from developing hard skills, but classes tend to be much more difficult to find, so you may have to work with alternative educational channels and methods.

True Story *I always try to get a "team mom" on my team. This skill has nothing to do with gender and everything to do with relatability. The team mom is the person who remembers everyone's birthday, arranges lunches and parties, commiserates when something goes wrong, and just generally makes the team feel like a family. I'll take a lesser technical skill any day if I can get a team mom (and I only need one per team). This person holds the team together and always knows when something is going wrong. As a project manager or manager I have to maintain schedules and discipline, but the team mom can be entirely understanding and sympathetic. The team mom is usually an important source of information for me, but even if that's not the case, the team mom helps my team function well.*

TRY IT

Let me show you what I mean with an exercise in team creation.

You're starting a new project to create a technology product. You need to choose the leads for each area. Let's code-name this project Stampede. (Code names are often used for projects requiring secrecy, but even when that's not required, a code name can be a source of identity and motivation for your team.) The profile of Stampede looks like this:

- The project is technically complex.
- The technology must integrate with a number of other technologies (and technology groups), both existing and under development, at your company.
- The project is likely to be fairly intense and highly visible.
- Some secrecy is required early on, but the product will be announced before it is complete and will be demoed at trade shows prior to completion.

You need three leads for Stampede: a technical lead, a product manager, and a QA lead. Here are your candidates:

Technical Lead Candidates

Pat	Syd
Experienced lead	Experienced lead but has not led a highly visible product
Very technical	Very technical
Abrupt manner (but tolerated due to technical adeptness)	Works well with others
Considered a leader in the field	Excellent communicator

Who would you choose? I would choose Syd in this situation. Both candidates are very technical, which is critical for this project (that seems like a hard skill, but it's generalized and implies an ability to spin up quickly on new technologies). Remember, though, that this team has to integrate with other products under development, which means establishing good relationships with the other team leads and communicating constantly. An abrupt communicator like Pat might be tolerated but would be less likely to build and maintain the relationships necessary to integrate well with multiple teams.

Product Manager Candidates

(Product managers define the product and typically represent it to the rest of the world, introducing it at trade shows, training sales organizations, and communicating with potential consumers of the product.)

Casey	Riley
Experienced presenter	*Deep understanding of technology*
Good understanding of technology	*Good technical communications (able to communicate technical details and understand engineers' conversation) and produces good technical documentation*
Excellent understanding of users of technology	*Respected by engineers*
Unflappable	*Largely inward facing (works within the company, not with customers)*
Generates good requirements	

Who would you choose? I would choose Casey for this kind of project. Casey doesn't have as deep an understanding of the technology, but I'm getting a high-end team lead who can work with

Casey to fill in any gaps. It's a fast-moving project, so good requirements from the start will help us meet the aggressive deadlines. An excellent understanding of the consumers of the technology is important in bleeding-edge development and helps reduce rework as the technical landscape changes. A general calmness will help keep the team focused. Finally, the product manager is going to be demonstrating unfinished technology to potential customers, so the ability to present well and deal with things going wrong during demonstrations is critical to market acceptance (and therefore to the success of the project and product).

QA Lead Candidates

Jessie	Jackie
Excellent QA knowledge and demonstrated ability	Good QA knowledge and demonstrated ability
Somewhat adversarial relationship with engineers	Recognized as a team builder
Technically adept	Go-to person for team members with issues
Able to automate testing	Technically conversant

Who would you choose? I'd choose Jackie. Jackie is good at QA. Technical adeptness would be useful, but in a high-pressure situation I would find a team builder of more value. Jackie understands the technology well enough to pull the QA team as well as the larger team together, and we can bring in highly technical QA engineers to deal with the details. Finally, while test automation is highly valuable in general, there won't be time to do that kind of work in this project, so that skill, which might be critical on another project, would be wasted in this one.

Starting to get the general idea?

TRY IT AGAIN

Let's see what happens on a different project with the same candidates.

You're trying to staff a new project, Nucleus. This is a highly technical project. It will form the core technology of the future products in your company. It uses bleeding-edge technologies, but the output of the project needs to be very stable. The internal workings must be kept confidential, and it must provide a set of functions that new products will use under the covers. As a reminder, here are your candidates:

Technical Lead Candidates

Pat	Syd
Experienced lead	Experienced lead but has not led a highly visible product
Very technical	Very technical
Abrupt manner (but tolerated due to technical adeptness)	Works well with others
Considered a leader in the field	Excellent communicator

Product Manager Candidates

Casey	Riley
Experienced presenter	Deep understanding of technology
Good understanding of technology	Good technical communications and documentation
Excellent understanding of users of technology	Respected by engineers
Unflappable	Largely inward facing
Generates good requirements	

QA Lead Candidates

Jessie	Jackie
Excellent QA knowledge and demonstrated ability	Good QA knowledge and demonstrated ability
Somewhat adversarial relationship with engineers	Recognized as a team builder
Technically adept	Go-to person for team members with issues
Able to automate testing	Technically conversant

Who would you choose for project Nucleus? Here are my picks: Technical Lead: Pat. This calls for someone extremely technical, even if a bit weak on communications (in fact, Pat will probably be less likely to accidently leak details than Syd for just that reason).

Product Manager: Riley. Nucleus is very technical and won't be visible on its own. The product manager needs to be quite technical to define the requirements so they're complete for use by the company's new products.

QA Lead: Jessie. This product needs to be as bulletproof as possible for software, and it requires technical depth to lead the quality effort. Jessie's adversarial relationship in this case will be an asset because it will likely keep the developers on their toes, and automating testing for a core component is always a good idea.

See how this works? The soft skills can really make a difference, based on the project needs.

Okay, so now you've staffed your project. You don't have a team yet; you just have a bunch of people assigned to work on the same project. Time to start getting the team moving like, well, a team.

TEAM IDENTITY

One way to build a team is to figure out your team's identity and make it part of your (and your team's) world. You won't be able to come up with a well-fitting identity until you've had your team together for a little while, so let it rattle around in your head a bit. This timing works out pretty well—about the time the team members have settled in and are maybe getting bored or restless you can pick things up with an identity. Once I had a team (five departments!) of project managers who I thought were ninjas. They all had a big list of projects, and they moved in and out of those lists knocking them down and moving on. At our monthly meetings, every project manager got a little ninja tchotchke for every project completed. When one of the project managers finished a huge, major project she got a cardboard cutout of Éowyn (from *The Lord of the Rings*—not exactly a ninja but definitely a warrior). It was a common theme and a way to help people who were operating largely independently feel like part of a bigger team.

Here's another example of a team identity. Have you ever seen the movie *Stripes*? There's a part where the (basic training army) unit is trying to get ready for an inspection drill, and they're fighting among themselves. Bill Murray's character gets them all together by noting that they're all "dogfaces" ("Look, his nose is cold!"). Then he asks them who cried at the end of *Old Yeller*. So now they're all dogfaces who cried at the end of a movie—they've agreed on something. Not only that, but they have an identity—they're the misfits, but it doesn't mean that they can't surprise everyone and do well in the inspection. And they do, but not exactly by the book.

Which leads us to another important reality regarding your team—they're not going to be like any team you've worked with before. You will have to understand how they work as a team to adjust your own processes to be most effective. (Yep, that's right; you have to change, not them.) This might mean that you need to adjust your communication style. It might mean that the standard processes need some tinkering to work best for this particular team. It's a good idea to put some processes and communication standards in place when you first start working with the team and then schedule some time to review and adjust once the team has actually become a team. Let your team know this is happening when you start, and make the team part of the review process. Once they understand that they'll get a chance to review, they'll spend more time figuring out what changes might work and less time resenting a process that feels wrong and imposed.

Everyone wants a say in decisions that affect them. Make that happen as often as you can, and the team will buy in. If there's a reason the team can't be involved in (or challenge) a decision, let them know why.

GOALS AND MOTIVATION

We've talked about individual goals and motivations and how to satisfy them whenever possible within the confines of the project. The team as an entity is no different. To keep your team together and on track, focus on the project goals. Be sure your four dials are identified (content, schedule, cost, and quality) with an emphasis on the goals for each. Have these goals front and center for every project meeting. Take the time to be sure that every person on your team understands each goal and her own part in it, and then get the team involved. (If you can have the team involved in creating the goals, or at least reviewing them, early in the project, you'll have better understanding and buy-in from them, but that's often not possible.) Be sure that you have regular explicit reviews of the goals to check that nothing has moved surreptitiously (because sometimes goals slide around without anyone noticing). Make the team responsible for meeting the goals; you're then responsible for keeping the team on track. All this makes a team more cohesive and creates a guide for resolving (and often avoiding) disagreements.

Knowing your team members' working styles and motivations can help you keep team interactions running smoothly. For example, pair someone who likes to learn with someone who likes to teach. Don't make people who snarl at each other work together one-on-one more than they need to.

GEOGRAPHICALLY DIVERSE TEAMS

It's increasingly rare for teams to be colocated (in other words, sitting all together). Tom DeMarco and Timothy Lister's book *Peopleware* explores the negative effect of even small distances (different floors or buildings).[1] Imagine how that translates now that so many teams are in different parts of the same country or different countries.

Fortunately, we have a whole new generation of tools to keep us connected and a whole new discipline of cultural intelligence.

Unfortunately, those tools will only help if we put in the time to work with the people using the tools. So once again we're reliant to some extent on individual relationships. This physical separation can have such an impact and requires so much additional attention that I've put in a whole chapter to help deal with it (see Step 8). For now, just realize that physically separated teams will require a bit more attention and a few new tools. As you start building your team, keep in mind that people in other locations will need to feel like part of the team (so don't ignore them when you're dealing with team interactions, goals, and soft skills).

SIGNS OF TOXICITY

Sometimes teams turn toxic. Nothing seems to go right, no one is happy, people aren't working together, and eventually the project starts to fall apart. Once that happens it's really hard to get everyone back to work and productive, so you'll need to watch for signs that the team is moving in the direction of dysfunction.

If people aren't helping each other and the schedule is reasonable, your team may be turning toxic. It's turned into every man for himself. If the schedule is unreasonable and people are punished for missing their deadlines (as opposed to the team taking the blame together if a milestone is missed), you might be setting up a toxic condition, so be sure there are appropriate rewards and incentives in place for helping other team members.

If the first response of most of the team in an emergency is to try to assign blame, your team may be turning toxic. Be sure that you lead response teams in root cause analysis and actual response, not trying to figure out who (instead of what) is responsible. The team is responsible (and ultimately you are responsible) for issues. You're responsible for ensuring a reasonable reaction and following up on both process and human error.

If you have trouble getting the team into meetings together and you're following my guidelines for productive meetings, check the temperature of the team and the project. If you can get them into meetings, but it seems that most of the discussions turn into squabbles without a resolution, you may need to take action.

If even your get-together food deliveries (see Step 9) have everyone grabbing something and running away, either your project is in trouble (people are trying desperately to get things done to meet an aggressive schedule) or they really don't want to sit down and eat with each other. Either way, you need to respond.

If most of your discussions with individual team members turn into complaint sessions about the team and its members, you need to turn those discussions around to what can be done or changed. Everyone grumbles from time to time, but if that grumbling has turned into the team and its members' modus operandi, you will need to try to get them back on track.

Sometimes, if you miss the warning signs or if the team has suddenly and completely fallen apart, you may need to call in an expert. Coaches who specialize in toxic teams will come in for a day session to work things out. If you feel you're at this point, get your ducks in a row with respect to all the signs of toxicity, what you've done to try to contain it, how you believe it's affecting productivity, and the likely cost to the project (in extra time, overtime, rework, missed sales, etc.) to present your case for a specialist to management.

Sometimes you step into a toxic environment. This could be the entire company or just your team's little part of it. When that happens you basically have three options. First, you can call it a day. Step out of the environment if you don't think it can be salvaged. Second, you can try to fix it. This is usually most possible when the problem is localized rather than existing across the whole company. Fixing it will probably involve work outside just your team (we've already addressed the team aspect). You'll have the best results if you can gather a few like-minded people and band together to find solutions. Finally, you can do your best to shield your team. (You can and should do this even if you're trying to fix the problem.) That means that you limit their exposure to the source of the toxicity, which may result in you attending meetings with people outside the team when you'd usually have members of your team working with other teams. It means that you intercept messages that will disrupt and/or demoralize your team and either deal with those items yourself or spin them to your team in a way that will cause the least angst. And it means that you step up your efforts to be both the face of your team to the rest of the world and the defender of the team.

True Story *Just before a big tech bubble burst, my start-up was acquired by another company. The company we joined operated in a very different way than my acquired company, so I worked with the managers to get some team building going and get people working with each other. We were making good progress when that bubble burst, and there were big layoffs and reorganizations in the company. I inherited a new team of five or six departments, many of them technical support functions. Product engineering and QA were outsourced, which left a lot of empty spaces in our office. Company and product direction changed on almost a daily basis. I worked on the last two options for dealing with a toxic environment, trying to fix it and shielding my team. I met often with the outsourced management and the executives, and I reported back news that was useful to my group. I helped establish connections between individual contributors on my team and individual contributors on other teams to keep moving forward and keep my folks out of the fray. And I provided a safe haven: I had an open door to everyone on the team, regular one-on-one meetings with my managers, and department meetings where everyone was free to say whatever he felt needed saying. Eventually, most of us left in another big layoff, but at least the time we spent in the chaotic environment was made tolerable. I think if market conditions had been different, we might have been able to work our way out of the toxicity eventually, so the attempt was valid (and even if it never brought about a real reduction in toxicity, the people on my team knew the effort was being made).*

WORKING WITH OTHER TEAMS

Teams rarely work in a vacuum. We often need things from other teams to move forward on our projects, and other teams need things from us. The other teams have personalities too, and it's easy to get tripped up if we communicate with them in ways that they don't like.

I have a set of questions I try to answer before I approach another team (or team lead) to be sure I don't start off on the wrong foot. If I can't get the answers before approaching the other team, I try to get them pretty quickly as I go along so we continue to have good communications and establish a good relationship.

Who is the leader? I want to know both the official leader and the leader in practice. Those aren't always the same person. Sometimes the official leader delegates responsibility; other times someone else in the group is more experienced, works behind the scenes, or for some other reason holds the real power or leadership role for the team. I'll need to work with both, but I have to understand who can best get things accomplished.

What's the best way to approach the group? Maybe email is their forte. Or maybe I'll need to have formal scheduled meetings with them. I'd like to know whether they work best in person or by phone (if they're not in my physical area it might be worth a trip to meet face-to-face once or at least to do some videoconferencing). I also want to know what tone to take with the group. Maybe they like things to be very businesslike and official, or maybe they like a friendly handshake kind of approach. If they do best with a hierarchical approach, I'll start with a bit of name-dropping or making my authority level clear in my interactions.

What are the group's motivators? Sometimes I even review my own materials on motivators to have a kind of ready list. Maybe they like extending their reach; maybe they like being part of a bigger project; perhaps they like to be in an advisory role or would like to teach me about their group, activities, customers, and processes. The more I know about how they work and respond, the better.

What does the group need? This could be anything from physical resources to trade-offs of tasks to public recognition to formal requests so they can account for their time. If I'm going to take their time working with me, I want to provide them whatever I can in return.

How (and how fast) does the group respond? I need to know in general how quickly I can expect a response when I make a request. This will help me understand what method they use for response (so I can set it up in advance)—email, meetings, phone calls, a ticket system, or whatever their processes and preferences call for. I'd also like to have an idea of how many responses it takes to get a real answer. Some groups do a lot of procrastinating, some groups trickle out information a bit at a time, some groups prefer to provide a full formal answer all at once, and some will provide an estimated time for response after they do an initial analysis. Some groups, unfortunately, will just ignore a request unless they're reminded on a very regular basis.

How willing is the group to work with other teams? This varies a great deal from group to group. Corporate, national, and group culture all play into the answer. The group's history will also influence whether they're really willing to work with other teams. Their schedule and other pressures may make it very difficult for them to spare time for other groups. Some teams are very insular and protect their knowledge, so knowledge sharing isn't something they're anxious to be part of. All this will factor into the way I approach and work with a team and what I'll be expecting from them.

How willing is the group to take responsibility for actions, tasks, and results? This will guide much of my format and interaction plan. If they're really on top of things, then meeting notes will probably be quite sufficient. If they forget things, like to play the blame game, or are so overloaded that things get lost on their to-do lists, I'll need to be more proactive in tracking—and nagging.

When should I escalate? Some groups expect an escalation to their management for requests so that management can make a priority call. Other groups consider escalation a last resort, so I'll need to treat it that way.

What's the best way to remind the group they owe me something? I want to know who to remind (and who to copy), how to remind (email? Phone calls? Skype?), what tone to use (businesslike, cajoling, annoyed), and how often to nag. The how often is really important to being able to walk that line between being annoying enough to put them off and not annoying enough to get into their queue.

Who is important to have in what kind of meetings? Maybe I need to have the manager or team lead in all the meetings. Maybe the whole group needs to be in on every meeting (yes, that would be annoying, but we do what's necessary for our projects). Maybe one-on-one works best. Sometimes agreements made with one team member turn out to be invalid, especially if the lead or manager likes to be directly involved.

What kind of documentation is needed? I always document meetings, but sometimes that's not enough. Perhaps I'll need to document informal discussions, at least with respect to agreements made. Maybe a wiki post of upcoming due dates is necessary to be sure everyone can see them. Perhaps I need to provide a weekly reminder of decisions and action items.

You can see that there's quite a bit of information that can be used to tailor good interactions with another group. Obviously, knowing as much as possible before the first contact can get you off to a much better start than you might otherwise have, so try to find folks you know have worked with the group before to give you some insight. Sometimes I just ask some of these questions point blank in my first meeting with the group.

It seems like a lot, but you can probably answer all these questions about your own team already and take a good shot at the answers for any team you work with regularly.

KEEP THE BEAT AND PUT ON YOUR PARTY HAT

We're Working Well; How Do I Keep It Going?

Okay, you've connected with the individuals on your team. You've connected with your team and connected them with each other. The team is working together, and everything is going smoothly. Are you done yet?

Nope. Like anything else, keeping your team working together takes work. Some of it is just part of the general project flow, some is pretty easy to work into the daily or weekly routine, and some requires some extra planning.

A word you'll see over and over in this section is "fun." Remember the statistic about how much faster we learn if we're having fun? It's important to incorporate that wherever you can. Sometimes you'll have to justify yourself to your management if you have managers who think fun is the opposite of productivity. Use that statistic on learning. Note how much faster, how many fewer defects, how much less absenteeism there is if people are happy at work. Try to put the result of celebrations and fun at work into terms of benefits to the project and the business. We know that people are more productive and make fewer errors, that there's less attrition, and that people are more willing to give the extra effort in an environment that they enjoy. Other than purely altruistic motivations, there are concrete benefits to providing a fun work environment.

MEETINGS AGAIN

Let's start with the easiest ways to keep your team working well together. You have regular meetings, and these are excellent times to evaluate and work with the team. First, follow the meeting rules we talked about in Step 4. Having team members actually show up for team meetings is an important part of team unity. Timing of meetings can help sustain the team flow. Meet often enough with good enough reason not to lose touch, but don't waste your team's time. Use team meetings to recognize good work by individuals or groups within the teams, and tie this recognition into the team identity. You'll also want to recognize team milestones and efforts on a regular basis. That means you need to pay attention to good things people do, make a note of them, and bring them up at an opportune time. You'll probably have some superstars who are easy to recognize and reward, which is fine, but you need to put in the effort to notice small victories and improvements from all members of your team. Depending on your team's personality, you may want to provide time in your meetings for team members to recognize each other. Encourage those team members who are uncomfortable with recognizing peers to let you know who they feel deserves recognition so you can provide it. In all of this remember motivations, and don't recognize team members in public if that embarrasses them. (One way around this restriction is to recognize several people at once so it feels more like team recognition than singling out an individual.)

ONGOING TEAM BUILDING AND
MAINTENANCE

You don't have to rely on big events to keep your team feeling like a team.

One good way to help your team stay connected is to **foster expertise**. Remember, everyone is good at something. Your first step is to figure out what that something is and its relationship to the project. This isn't always easy. You'll need to establish a relationship with each individual to discover her expertise (those questions about weekend activity can help, as can asking what she enjoyed about previous jobs and assignments). Once you know what everyone is good at, recognize each one for it. Ask each person if he could be the contact for those on the team needing help in his area of expertise, and then advertise that expertise and availability in your team meetings. Perhaps have each person give a short presentation on their area of expertise in a team meeting. (Don't do this all in one meeting; keep it short and think about one presentation per meeting.) Advertise on your intranet or team web page the expertise you have on your team so team members can easily figure out where to go when they need help.

Once you have your **team identity** you can use that to help solidify the team relationships. Use it on your materials—your team web page, meeting agendas and minutes, wherever you can find that seems like a good vehicle. Think about getting tchotchkes (little figures, patches, whatever you can find) for everyone that represents the team identity. If you have the budget, look into T-shirts that have a connection to the team identity. (Important note: Get everyone's size ahead of time. It's pretty demotivating if you think you're a size small and your project manager gets you a large. Never default to extra large for everyone. I have lots of T-shirts that immediately became rags because they could fit three of me, and every one of them made me feel like I wasn't important enough to even size a T-shirt. These are seemingly innocuous shortcuts that have the potential to sabotage your relationships.) Think about a team mascot you can pass around when people do something good. All these things not only reinforce the identity; they bring some fun to the project.

If you have people on your project who don't interact much in their day-to-day work, you need to find ways to **pair them up** in other situations. If there's nothing much intersecting on the work front, get creative. For example, product managers and quality engineers may not interact much from a work perspective. You can do something as simple as asking the two of them to go pick up lunch or to put a presentation together.

Create a **team web page** and link it to the project web page. On the team page put a picture of each person on the team (it should be a real representation, not an avatar of any sort, because these pictures will help people get familiar with each other, particularly if they're in different locations). Add a profile for each person, including work-related information like title, role on the team, and areas of expertise, but ask each person for one non-work piece of info they'd like others on the team to know about them. That one thing might be about the person's family, pets, hobbies—anything that gives a clue to the whole person. You can also put team-building event pictures on or linked to this page.

It's up to you to **be a cheerleader** for your team. Recognize both personal and professional achievements, and applaud jobs well done. Encourage other team members to do the same, either privately or publicly. One of my first questions when a team member praises another team member in a meeting with me is whether she told the other team member that she appreciated the effort. (Hint: The answer is usually something along the lines of "No, but that would probably be good, huh?")

Finally, **develop team customs**. These can be as big as handing out personalized awards at the end of a project (based on whatever each person was best at or contributed most), or as small as the ninjas marking milestones. These create even more of a team identity, allowing everyone to participate and marking another thing special and particular to *this* team.

True Story *I was the first person to take a vacation at a start-up. I was celebrating both a milestone birthday and the completion of my master's degree, so my family and I went to the Club Med in the Dominican Republic. When I came back to work my cubicle was decorated with tropical reminders (colorful nets, an inflatable palm tree, some sand and shells—you get the idea). The explanation was that the team wanted to ease my reentry into the real world. That immediately became a custom; every time someone went on vacation he came back to a cubicle decorated in the style of the vacation destination.*

TEAM-BUILDING EVENTS

Events can make a team out of a group of people fast. The trade-off (because there's always a trade-off) is that team-building events take thought and planning as well as some time away from the project. It's usually a reasonable trade-off for getting your team functioning well.

We all want to start things off with a bang, but it's better to know a bit about your team before you sponsor an event. Use a more standard kickoff (but make it fun) to start your project while you get a handle on the personality of your new team. The better you understand both the individuals and the team, the more effectively you can plan your event. (And there's no need to stop at one event. If you have a long project, you may want to do more team-building events to keep the energy level up.)

Movies, amusement parks, arcades, and the like are not good team-building events. I know you're asking why—these events are easy to plan and execute! This kind of activity is great for a reward or pick-me-up, but not for team building. Movies mean no interaction among team members until it's over (or else there will be a lot of shhh-ing), although if you have a group meal afterward and get a discussion going you can make it work as a minievent. Amusement parks and arcades encourage people to scatter, often in small groups or even (shudder) cliques. You need to find something interactive that requires everyone to participate. A team-building event should encourage working together as well as providing a shared experience (although sometimes, particularly when the energy level is low, the shared experience without a lot of work is a better choice).

Problem-solving excursions are great team-building events. Scavenger hunts (have them come back with pictures; don't have people bringing license plates back the way we did when we were kids!), locked rooms, and ropes courses all work really well. They encourage both cooperation and in some cases competition between groups within the team (assign people who don't know each other or haven't worked closely together).

Don't limit yourself to competitions and problem-solving, though. Shared experiences can work as well as problem-solving, especially experiences that few or no team members have had before.

Be aware of any physical limitations of team members. Everyone can't do everything, and nothing will torpedo team building like leaving someone out. Think twice about paintball (a perennial favorite), ropes courses, or anything with a very physical component before you schedule it. If *everyone* on the team is up for it, then you're good.

True Story *A large, long project finished after three years. We had people coming to Santa Cruz, California, from Toronto and London as well as lots of locals. We were looking for something new that everyone would like. After discarding paintball (we thought twice), we considered* a local steam train ride through the redwoods during which bandits on horseback would rob the train, with a BBQ at the end of the ride. That became the runner-up, but the winner was a kayaking trip through Elkhorn Slough (a local nature preserve on the Pacific Ocean) led by a naturalist. It wasn't too strenuous, and we stopped partway through for a picnic lunch. The few people who didn't want to paddle a kayak were able to take a ride with another naturalist to the lunch point. People remembered this one for years.

Another True Story *After several days of planning sessions with folks from Europe and the U.S. Midwest and West Coast, we were looking for something unique to do for a break. We offered several choices of activities in and around Silicon Valley before we scheduled anything, including a trip to the Tech Museum in Silicon Valley and special tours of the Winchester Mystery House in San Jose. The winner, hands down, was a tour at Año Nuevo when the elephant seals were onshore and the babies were learning to swim. Even many of the local team members hadn't been there before. The tour involved several miles of nonstrenuous walking, which everyone was able to do. Unfortunately, it also happened during a particularly wet winter. It was cold, rainy, and windy when we went. (As a project manager, I of course had a contingency plan; I had rain ponchos for everyone ready to go ahead of time.) We went. Everyone was soaked, but it was prime elephant seal weather, and the big bulls were moving around. All the local elementary school groups had canceled because of the weather, so we were able to do a few things that would have been more dangerous to children if they'd been around, and we were able to get incredibly close to the animals. By the end, despite the ponchos, everyone was soaked, cold, and tired but exhilarated. It was a once-in-a-lifetime experience that everyone remembers (and we have the pictures to prove it).*

Yet Another True Story *This story doesn't have a happy ending, but it's instructive nonetheless. My start-up had been acquired by another company and there was a team-building event scheduled to help us get to know each other. We went go-kart racing at an indoor track. It* was fun for many of us, with small teams competing, but there were people who couldn't (or were afraid to) participate. These people were left out and had to watch. It was dangerous (you had to wear a full fire suit as well as helmet and neck-roll, and the borders were hay bales and tires). Large people (of which there were several) didn't fit in the karts, and short people ended up with bruised legs because they had to rest calves on part of the steering mechanism. A great event for those who were comfortable with it all but really off-putting and isolating for those who couldn't. (Note: I've been to other go-kart events where everyone was pretty happy about it. The venue of the event wasn't a problem, but the research into the team members was.)

TRY IT

You have a new team:

- The team is not communicating well, causing miscues and rework.
- A few members have worked together before and tend to work mostly with each other.
- There are 12 team members, all colocated.
- All members are mobile, ages 25 to 50.
- Budget is $100 per person.
- One day can be allocated to this event.

What will you plan?

There are a number of things you'll need to take into consideration. If the team is not working well, you need to remove them from their work environment. If they are forming into cliques, you need to get them in an environment where they work with team members who aren't in their groups. You have a reasonable budget and people who can move around. Look into things like ropes courses, small-group escape rooms, or scavenger hunts. Don't even think about movies, theme parks, or allowing people to choose their own group for an exercise. Think about box lunches so there's no excuse for team members to sit at a table with their usual cohorts.

FIGHTING BURNOUT

Burnout can be a problem in the best and most high-performing teams, and we need to keep a close watch for it. Everyone is pretty aware that extended bouts of overtime lead to burnout, if for no other reason than lack of sleep, but plenty of other factors can contribute to a case of team burnout.

Like a lack of motivation, burnout can be contagious and infect your whole team even if only one person is suffering. There's a domino effect where those not initially affected start picking up tasks from those having trouble, which overloads more people, etc.

You can control and combat many of the factors that contribute to burnout with regular team-building activities and celebrations. The best and easiest way to keep your team from burning out is to avoid creating an environment where people are fatigued.

Controlling overtime is the obvious factor. Good, solid project management is the best source of this control, coupled with effective business relationships. Good project management means that you have realistic schedules and regular check-ins as well as constant risk assessment, so you have early warning of potential issues. Effective business relationships will ensure that you're aware of the risks and know if anyone is having trouble completing tasks on time.

Beware of challenging people beyond their capacity or in areas that represent significant risk to the project. Many people like a challenge, but if you put them in a position where their response to the challenge will make or break the project, you've put them in a very stressful and highly avoidable situation.

Especially watch those people on your team who are very helpful; they may endanger their own work in the course of helping others. You may need a more granular task breakdown to help the helpful stay on track and avoid overextending themselves helping others.

Repetitive projects with no discernible milestones, as are often encountered with an Agile process, can burn people out. These projects don't have the big events present in more traditional process models, and that can make a project seem never ending and relentless. Be sure to make some milestones for any Agile or repetitive project, and celebrate achieving those milestones. Move people around to work on different projects so there's at least a change of scenery. Challenge people with new aspects of the project where you can. After all, an Agile iteration is a short period of time, so the risk of the challenge is pretty well contained.

Above all, remember that a short-term work stoppage ("Everyone take tomorrow off") will pay off handsomely in higher productivity after the short break. In the midst of a project it often seems like you can't afford the time, but if your team is suffering from burnout, you're already losing significant productivity, which means you're dealing with a significant risk to schedule and quality.

YOU! CALL 911!

I've been CPR certified since I was in high school. That means I've had to recertify every three years, and I've seen a lot of changes in the CPR process during that time.

Once cell phones became ubiquitous the process changed. At that point we were instructed to call out, "Someone call 911," before we waded into a situation. The next time I certified after that, this instruction had changed. The process was (and remains) to point at a particular person and say, "You, call 911."

So why the change? It's because there's a weird group dynamic that shows up with nonspecific instructions to a group: no one picks up the assignment. I have no idea why this is; maybe everyone assumes someone else is doing it, or maybe no one wants to step outside her perceived authority. Whatever the reason, it happens in all kinds of situations.

This is a real blind spot for most of us project managers. If we're not the ones heading into the situation to help, we're already on our phones calling 911. That difference in our behavior versus the behavior of most (non-project-managing) people means that we sometimes make poor assumptions about group behavior. Those assumptions can cause some real issues, as assumptions so often do.

The lesson from this is to always make an assignment specific. It doesn't matter if a team of people will work on it; put a point person in the position of responsibility. This is why we put names (and dates) on action items. Calling a group the owner of a task is not much different from having no owner.

True Story *A new project manager was implementing a version of an application for a new site. She provided the test plan to the group of users responsible for evaluating the implementation and told them they needed to complete testing within two weeks. They all nodded their head when she gave the instruction in a meeting. Two weeks later, absolutely no testing had been done. In the next meeting the project manager reissued the test plan to the group, but this time with a person's name next to each item. (She felt kind of silly doing this but was game enough to try it anyway.) A week later, all the testing was complete, along with extra testing that had been done as people got into the system and decided to test areas they were particularly interested in. No one had any problems with doing the testing. The odd group dynamic had just kicked in on the first test plan, and nothing got done until there were names on the tasks.*

HOW GOOD ARE THEY REALLY?

Sometimes people actually have a different level of skill, particularly with hard skills, than they believe they have. This break with reality can have serious consequences for your team. Here's how it works.

The first problem is when someone isn't good at something but he believes he is. In other words, he's oblivious. Obviously, from a project standpoint this means that things will start falling behind. From a team standpoint, other people are either picking up after this person or watching the project stumble. Neither is going to help morale. People who believe they have more skill than they actually do are generally pretty happy people, so we're often reluctant to burst their bubble in the hopes that a miracle will occur and they'll suddenly be as good as they think they are. You're going to have to address this head on, not wait for the universe to help you out to keep your team intact and your project on track. The first thing you'll need to do is talk to the person, armed with the evidence that his skills are not at a level to succeed in the project. Focus on the work product, not the person, as evidence. Give the person some time to absorb it (because he'll suddenly be at a different point in his self-evaluation), and then walk through options. Can you arrange some classes or mentoring to bring the person up to speed? Are there other tasks on the project that this person can do to trade work around the team? Talk to the person before you approach management because there may be a good solution that works for the team. As always, do this in private. Your team will know it's been addressed; there's no need to do it publicly.

The next kind of problem you might run into is that someone isn't up to speed and she knows it. These people are nervous, fearful, and sometimes angry. You'll encounter this situation when someone has recently been promoted or has been given assignments that use a newly obtained skill. Add schedule pressure, and you have a potentially volatile situation. For these people, you first need to let them know you understand. Get a plan together to improve or practice the skill. If necessary, have them reestimate their tasks so they feel they've had input and so that you have a realistic schedule.

The perfect situation is when you have someone who is exactly good at something as they think they are, and their tasks are assigned appropriately for their skill level. Eventually, everyone moves out of this level to either trying something new or advanced or to being a superstar (which brings its own problems), so be watchful while you enjoy the peace.

The final problem is when you have a superstar and she doesn't realize she's a superstar. She assumes that everyone is as good as she is and becomes impatient when people don't seem to be paying attention or are moving too slowly. This manifests as a kind of arrogance that can cause a lot of resentment among other team members. You're going to have to sit this person down and explain the situation to her. Tell her that everyone is very good at *something*, but let her know that the something is not necessarily the skill in question. What you want to get to is an understanding with her that people are listening but that your superstar is talking too fast.

True Story *I was a project manager at a large company that had retraining programs for scarce skills, allowing people whose jobs were becoming obsolete to move on to something of more value to the company. The retraining programs were also used as incentives to challenge high performers looking for a new kind of career. I'd worked with several people coming out of these programs, and they were usually eager to do well and quite competent; however, on one project I was assigned Jill, who didn't fit that profile. Jill had always wanted to be a programmer and leapt at the chance to make the transition. I never did know what Jill did before she was a programmer, but apparently whatever it was, she did it very well. Programming, however, was Jill's dream job—the problem was that she just couldn't do it. She couldn't write the most basic of programs without help and had no clue how to test them. Others on the team helped her—a lot—but it was clear she wasn't able to do the job. She got more and more upset and angry, so it was difficult for the team to work with her. I talked with her, but at that point in my career I wasn't experienced enough to see the warning signs early or to approach her in a way that would keep her listening. By the time I* tried to address the problem, the project was behind and the rest of the team was getting annoyed. While management worked through the problem, the only way I could get the team calmed down and the schedules realistically set was to estimate Jill as being a negative 1.5 people—because not only would she not produce much of use, she'd use up half another person's time to do it. Management supported that planning while they worked things out, the team could see what was going on without actually putting a negative number in the schedule (I adjusted schedules for all the people who would be helping Jill and let them know about it), and Jill was at least not as unhappy or disruptive. At the end of the project Jill moved on and eventually out of programming. You're not always going to be able to improve someone's skill if they don't have the basic aptitude or don't believe the skill needs improvement, but you may still need to accommodate that person while creating realistic schedules and satisfying your team.

Another True Story In a different company on a different project, I had an absolute superstar of a software engineer, Julio. He was young, eager, and impatient. The rest of the team was actually quite advanced and very good at software engineering, but Julio was in another class altogether. The team was becoming restless as Julio got more impatient with the work and with explaining what he was doing. I took him aside to talk to him about the situation. His response was one that I've heard several times since with high performers—he wanted to know if he was just supposed to assume that no one was as good as he was. He wasn't arrogant, just talented, and this seemed like a bad idea to him. My response was that he only needed to assume that the other engineers weren't as quick as he was in this particular area, that every engineer on the team was overall an excellent software engineer and that every one of them had superstar skills in at least one area. I was able to enumerate some of these skills so he could understand. Julio immediately caught on and began watching the other engineers handle situations in which they were more skilled than the rest of the team without becoming impatient. It was a good learning experience for Julio and a big step forward for the whole team.

So now you've established relationships with your team members, you're motivating the individuals, you've built (and are maintaining) a cohesive team, you've addressed and continue to address skills-perception mismatches, and your project is running smoothly. The next thing you need to worry about is keeping the team motivated. Team building is a great start, but celebrations are key to maintaining the team's motivation and forward motion.

Almost everyone has a celebration at the end of a project. That's a good thing, but it doesn't help on the way through. To keep up morale, keep some fun in the work, and show appreciation, it's important to celebrate all through a project.

MILESTONES

Every project has milestones. Whether that's completion of a phase, the end of a sprint, or the first successful software build doesn't matter. What does matter is that the team met a goal. You're already focusing your team on each milestone, just add a celebration when it's completed to your plan. Depending on the milestone, the team, the budget, and the degree of difficulty, your celebration could be as small as a cake in a team meeting or as large as an off-site event. Milestone celebrations are a time when you can (at least sometimes) use those activities that aren't as productive in team building—a group off-site to a movie, an arcade, things that are just meant to be fun. They don't have to be expensive, but it's important that they happen and that the team as a whole is recognized.

END-OF-PROJECT BLOWOUTS

The end-of-project celebration doesn't do a lot for morale during the project, but looking forward to that event can be motivating. This is especially true once you have a track record of great celebrations.

Once again, these don't have to be expensive. They do need to be fun. Invite senior management for at least part of it to tell the team how good their work was. As with team-building events, find something that everyone can enjoy. Be sure to hand out awards. These can be major, like monetary awards, but they don't have to be. If you can, give *everyone* on the team an award. Think carefully about what everyone contributed; at the very least you can give a personalized certificate with this information. It sounds small, but in reality it's a big deal to be recognized for what you're good at. If it's been a long, hard project involving a lot of overtime, you may want to have an event the families of your team members can attend.

RECOGNIZING PERSONAL AND TEAM TRIUMPHS

There are plenty of small victories in any project. It's important to recognize and celebrate these.

You can use the team identity to give tchotchkes or certificates or even things like chocolate bars for small victories—conquering a new technology, a successful test run or inspection, and the like. Be sure to give these in a team meeting so the team as a whole can celebrate. Remember the ninjas? Several people in that group (and it was a pretty large group, 30 people or so) rolled their eyes when I started giving out the ninjas. They felt that it wasn't serious and was just a distraction when they could have been working (at least one of them was a manager herself). After a few months they each came to me and said that, even though they initially thought it would be a waste of time, they could see the value and the building of morale that was coming out of it. This is often the case; everyone won't be on board initially, but if you keep at it without going overboard (and without expecting that everyone will like everything you try) you'll win people over.

Get into the habit of marking successes with celebrations small and large. This means that you have to actually notice these successes. Move on from the mind-set of "That's their job." It's true, finishing tasks on the project is each person's job, and I'm not advocating celebrating completion of every task in your project plan. Celebrating everything means nothing is really special, and part of the point of the celebration is to recognize something special. Give some serious thought to what kind of things you want to celebrate. Certainly, project milestones should get some recognition. Finishing a difficult or stressful task (one with a high risk, a lot of unknowns, difficult technical requirements) is usually cause for celebration; finishing that kind of task when it takes a team effort is especially worth celebrating.

Finding a better way to do something is a good thing to celebrate. You probably don't want to do this with the garden-variety small process improvements, but doing it for something that team members have taken the time to investigate, propose, and implement can be really valuable.

Once you have some idea of what kinds of things you'd like to celebrate, you're going to need to start looking for them. Review status reports with an eye to anything special or outstanding. Keep your eyes open for someone (or better yet, the whole team) going above and beyond.

Survival is a valid cause for celebration. Sometimes recovering from something that went wrong is a herculean effort that deserves a bit of cutting loose. (I still have a water bottle that says "App 2.0—because we're not dead yet!" which cleverly incorporated the engineering cultural favorite Monty Python.) Working through crises can either bring a team closer together or divide them with finger-pointing and frustration. It's up to you to be sure they land on the good side of that equation.

TRY IT

Think about these four situations. You're going to celebrate your success. How would the celebrations differ for these milestones?

1. You have finished a major project that had some issues, but overall has been a smooth project, on time and within budget. A follow-on will be coming soon. Your team is 20 people.
2. You've finished the first milestone in a new project. It was harder than expected to get people with the necessary skills for the team, and it took them a while to gel. The milestone came in pretty much on schedule but it was a struggle. Your team is 10 people.
3. You've finished an interim milestone in a medium-sized project. Your team is 25 people. There's plenty more ahead.
4. A group of people on the team has put in time researching an emerging industry process and found a way to apply it to your project that saves effort and improves quality.

ANSWERS
(OR AT LEAST SOME FOOD FOR THOUGHT):

1. Finishing a major project is a big deal. If there's a follow-on project coming with the same team, you need to plan ahead, otherwise the overlap will be a problem. You need to take the time to celebrate before the next phase gears up. Your team needs a bit of downtime. In this kind of situation we sometimes think that a pat on the back is all that's needed because we have to get to work on the next phase, but that kind of thinking will get you a burned-out team in a hurry. Do something big, be sure there's individual as well as team recognition, and get off the work site for an entire day. Even if there's a next phase, if the budget permits you should mark this completion with something—shirts, jackets, plaques, awards, whatever you can manage to say thank you.

2. Milestone celebrations are smaller in scope but just as important. Especially if you have a team that's just now coming together and they're coming off a hard milestone, you want to be sure to mark the milestone. In general, an off-site lunch, a tchotchke, and maybe the rest of the afternoon off will fit the bill for this kind of situation.

3. After the team meets an interim milestone, you want to recognize the effort in and completion of the milestone and get the team used to being appreciated when they finish something big. Even an on-site party, with food and possibly some recognition from the customer or upper management, will help keep your team motivated.

4. Finding something that saves effort and improves quality should definitely be recognized but doesn't really need a big

event. Bring a cake to a department meeting, get some publicity for the process and its application in a bigger forum (company newsletter or industry publication, for example), and maybe give a certificate to those who did the work.

KEEP CALM AND CARRY ON

Handle Emergencies Wisely

Stuff happens: projects go sideways, big mistakes are made, and crises occur. (If they didn't, we project managers would be out of a job.) How you handle setbacks, even with team members who trust you, can make or break your project. A misstep could ruin the relationship work you've been doing.

KEEPING OUT OF TROUBLE TO BEGIN WITH

To avoid trouble, be sure you do your risk analysis. Take a look every week and make sure contingency plans are in place for anything big. If you don't have contingency plans that everyone knows about (that's right, just making them for documentation's sake doesn't help), you'll have plenty of heroes who leap into action when there's a problem. If that happens, you really will have a nasty case of cat herding to work on. People will do stuff off the top of their head to try to fix the issue. They won't write down what they did (so won't remember it all) and probably won't tell you they did anything (well, unless the fix works and they can be heroes), and you'll be in worse shape than you were when you started. Trying to unravel the results of a panic can be painful. So do your homework.

Good prep will cut down on the number of ways a project can go wrong and will make it easier to respond when it does, but good preparation rarely avoids every possible issue.

WHAT TO DO WHEN TROUBLE FINDS YOU

First, don't panic. (Remember to breathe.) Second, don't point fingers and don't let anyone else start down the blame path.

If you have a contingency plan for the issue, it's best to call a meeting immediately. If for some reason that's not going to work, send an email triggering the contingency plan. In either case, remind everyone where to find the contingency plan and who's doing what, and tell everyone when and how to report status. After that, the process is largely the same as what to do when you don't have a plan. Skip ahead to the section "Fix the Problem."

If you don't have a contingency plan for the issue, immediately rally the troops. Send out a message for everyone to keep their hands off their keyboards (or hammers or whatever they'll use to try to help) and get them into a meeting together. In that meeting, first clearly state the problem so everyone is working on the same issue. (You might be surprised at how many versions of a single situation can exist in your team if you don't set a baseline.) Everyone will want to do something—anything—to fix the issue, so you'll need to calm them down and be sure you have a root cause analysis (or that the team is working on one). Responding to emergencies is a combination of basic project management and process analysis, but everyone on your team is not a project manager or process analyst. Most people are inherently helpful and prone to panic, and you'll need to corral that help instead of letting people set off on their own.

When you talk about the problem, specifically address the process issues. Avoid blame. Even if someone did something really dumb, there's going to be a hole in the process that allowed the something dumb to happen without a failsafe. Work on fixing the problem, then work on ensuring the problem doesn't happen again.

If you are working on a root cause analysis, you're going to have to understand who did what leading up to the issue, but absolutely keep the discussion at that level. In other words, just the facts, ma'am. Don't assign blame, just get to work on the root cause.

Root Cause Analysis That Works

There are many ways to work on root cause analysis—Ishikawa diagrams, cause-effect diagrams, mind maps—but we're not here to talk about that kind of technique. What we're concerned about are the team dynamics and the minefields associated with people trying to get to an answer quickly in the face of an emergency.

The first imperative is that you have all the **right players** in the root cause analysis session. If you miss someone with something to contribute, you may not come up with the right answer (or any answer at all). Get the right people together, as many in the same room as you can.

Be prepared with the **right tools**. You're going to need a whiteboard or similar mechanism, and if you're working with a distributed team, you'll need videoconferencing ability or at least a whiteboard application.

Now that you've got everyone together, everyone can see what's going on. People are running on adrenaline and are going to want to jump right in. Don't let them do it.

It bears repeating: once you have the team assembled, **state the problem clearly**. Be sure everyone agrees on what the problem is. It seems like a given, but it never ceases to amaze me how often people in a root cause analysis session aren't working on the same problem.

You need to think like a two-year-old when you're doing root cause analysis. **Keep asking why**, why, why to get to the real cause. There will be a tendency to grab onto the first cause that seems reasonable, but that may be just a symptom or even a red herring that will just get you more emergencies and more sessions.

Avoid the blame game (I'm being repetitive, but it's important). If someone didn't do something she "should" have, look at why she didn't do it. Was there a hole in the checklist? (Was there a checklist at all?) Is there a process problem that led to the bad decision? If someone did something careless, you can address it with that person later; for now, you're just trying to find the reason the problem occurred.

If your team is not able to come up with the solution, you have some options. The first is to bring in someone who knows the general subject matter but isn't on this specific project—for example, if the problem seems to be with the database, bring in a database administrator not currently on the project to get a different view. Another technique is to bring in someone with no working knowledge of the project at all. Sometimes having to explain every step explicitly exposes poor assumptions or something people were looking past.

Fix the Problem

If the entire team should be involved in figuring out what to do next, by all means address that as soon as you're able. If you only need a subset of the team to formulate a response, let the rest of the team go, but be sure to keep them in the loop.

Once you have a course of action that has everyone on board (or at least paying attention), assign tasks. Have people report progress to you (tell them how often to send progress reports—hourly, when they've finished a task, at the end of the day, or whatever makes sense given the situation). The reporting may seem obvious to you, but it won't be to everyone. It will help ground the team.

You will then need to report consolidated progress to the entire team regularly. Remember that those on the team with no immediate tasks are going to get itchy and eventually try to jump in and help unless you're feeding them status and other information. It's very important to keep management in the loop in these cases as well (be assured they're going to call you if you don't keep them updated). Use your judgment to determine who needs updates at what point, but provide at least one general status to everyone on a regular basis.

Finally, call it done when it is. Generate a final report, and move on to the next step.

WHEN IT'S OVER

Whew! You got through it! Chances are that everyone is happy the situation is resolved, and they really don't want to talk about it anymore. Once the adrenaline wears off people will want to move on. If you let that happen, you'll find yourself in the same situation later. Now that you're past the immediate issue, determine whether you need a more extensive solution. You need to figure out how to keep the issue from reoccurring. Marshal those exhausted troops as soon as they've recovered, and keep them operating as a team.

You'll need a postmortem. (In the current terminology this postevent review is often called a retrospective, but I feel that "postmortem" is a much more descriptive term for what happens next. Words are important and help set the tone. I'll use the two terms interchangeably for this section.)

I don't want people coming into a postmortem to do a play-by-play, recounting every step along the way. I want people to come prepared to dissect the situation and response. The postmortem meeting is to dive into the problem (root cause analysis should already have been done, so this discussion will be more about warning signs and what might have been missed), talk about what went right and what went wrong, and decide what process changes are needed to avoid the situation in the future.

We're used to doing retrospectives after a release or iteration, but there are many other uses for this kind of meeting. Here's the best process to use to get productive results that actually improve your process.

After you clearly state the subject of the meeting, *start with what went right.* There's always at least one thing that went well in any situation. It's important to capture what went well so that you keep on doing it. Starting the meeting with what went right moves people into a better, less negative mind-set for the next part of the meeting: what needs improvement (okay, it's "what went wrong" but with a more positive attitude). If you've already performed a root cause analysis, this part will be fast; if you haven't, it may take a little more time.

Finally, determine what process changes need to be made to address the "needs improvement" items.

Now, most postmortems end here, which means that the process improvements typically are dead on arrival. Before you adjourn the meeting, assign each of the process improvements as an action item and set a date to get the team back together to review the changes implemented via these action items. Remember to assign a single person to each action item (You! Call 911!—see Step 6). This ensures that the process changes have an owner and are implemented and provides the team a nice sense of completion and accomplishment. It really helps counteract the aftereffects of an emergency.

WHAT IF IT WAS SOMEONE'S FAULT?

All this focus on process doesn't mean that you never address the people issues. It's true that there's generally a failsafe missing in a process that let someone make a mistake. It's also true that chastising people in a public forum is demoralizing to everyone; no one knows who you'll turn on next. On the flip side, if people on your team think someone has done something wrong and they've had to clean up—and that person got away with it—they won't trust you to do the right thing. The answer is that if someone is responsible for an issue, you need to address it. Privately. Your team will know; there's no need to tell them. The critical part here is that you do this last, but you do it. What you're looking for is accountability, not blame.

TRY IT

Addressing issues with individuals can be tricky. Remember the example in Step 1 about your operations expert ditching the on-call because his child was in the emergency room? Let's look at another scenario. This one is a team situation more than a project situation.

As a horse person, I've been in many barns. Some have had teen horsemanship programs in which the teenagers work around the barn and do groundwork with the horses as well as riding. Let's suppose you're running one of these programs. The kids are cleaning stalls this morning. You go into a horse's stall. It's clean, but there's a pitchfork on the stall floor. (Some background information: horses will not only step on a pitchfork and hurt themselves, many will spook if they step on an end and the fork handle pops up and hurt themselves running into things. Many more horses will get bored and start to play with the fork. Some horses manage to break the handle and subsequently impale themselves. All in all, letting implements in stalls is a very bad idea.)

You know that Sara was assigned to clean the stall. She's done this kind of thing before, and she tends to leave jobs undone if there's something more fun available.

What do you do?

MY ANSWER (YOUR MILEAGE MAY VARY)

First, I'd call the team together and ask who can tell me why it's a problem to leave a pitchfork in a stall when you step out. (This lets someone shine by knowing the answer and ensures that everyone is aware of the problem and why it's a problem.)

Some of the kids are going to immediately pipe up with "That was Sara." I'll ignore that, but I'll ask Sara to pick up the pitchfork and put it away.

A bit later in the day, I'll catch Sara away from the rest of the team. I'll let her know that the behavior is unacceptable and recount what could have happened (since fortunately nothing did this time). And then I'll let her know that for the next three weeks she won't be cleaning the stalls. Nope, she'll be emptying all the wheelbarrows from the other stalls being cleaned. (Making it easier for her to remember to do the right thing.)

Doing it this way, I've accomplished several things. I've let someone who didn't do the wrong thing shine by telling everyone what the dangers are. I've educated any new team member who might not have been aware of the potential dangers. I've had a talk with Sara and let her know it was a problem, but not in front of the whole team. They'll know; someone will have been watching, but more importantly they'll notice that she's dumping manure for the next three weeks. They know the problem was addressed, and they know that if they mess up, they won't be embarrassed in public. Finally, I've helped her remember the right thing by making doing the wrong thing pretty darn inconvenient.

A TOOL TO HELP AVOID REPEATING MISTAKES:
MAKE IT EASIER TO DO THE RIGHT THING

Speaking of doing the right thing, there's an easy little tool that comes from natural horsemanship (yep, horses again), and if you read the answer to the previous exercise, you've seen how it works: make it easier to do the right thing than it is to do the wrong thing. This is as effective with people as it is with horses (and dogs and cats; it's one of those very versatile tools).

The premise is that nearly everyone will take the easier path by default. In today's world we have so much coming at us and everyone is so busy that taking the easiest path is almost always the route of choice.

Sure, you can correct people. You can tell them why it's important to do things the right way. You can threaten and punish if they don't toe the line, but under pressure and time constraints they'll usually go back to the easier way of doing things.

Rather than spending the emotional capital of using a metaphorical stick, you can use this tool to avoid being the bad guy while still getting people to do things the right way.

It's very simple. Compare the desired behavior with the actual behavior and see if you can figure out why the actual behavior might be easier. Does the person need some education that he can't find the time for? Give him a quick private session and some notes on how to do it himself. Does the person dislike paperwork? Make the paperwork for doing paperwork the wrong way more onerous than that for doing it the right way. Is the process actually flawed? Do a quick process improvement effort, including this person in the improvement definition. (Ownership of a process and participation in its definition will often get people motivated to follow it or to go through the right channels to improve it.) Are you or someone else doing something for someone over and over when she should be doing it herself? Keep in mind that we often get in our own way on this front, enabling the very behavior we want to change.

As a general rule, when someone asks you to do something he should be doing and you think it's a one-time occurrence, do it. It happens—people get busy, something gets in the way, and it's sometimes quicker for you to do something once than to get them to do it. If, however, it's obvious that this is something that's going to happen again, pull out your handy make-it-easier tool and find a way to make it easier for the person to do it himself than ask you to do it.

As always, I have examples.

True Story *One company has a career path from internal customer support to project management. A new project manager, Maria, was trying to come up to speed. Maria had been a senior, knowledgeable, and very effective customer support lead—the go-to person in the department—before she became a project manager. The project managers sit very near the support department, and customer support representatives walked to where Maria was now working and regularly asked her customer support questions. She answered the questions but got more and more annoyed at the constant interruptions. From Maria's perspective these reps weren't doing their job, and they were affecting her project work. That was true, but it made sense if you looked at it from the customer support rep's view: he got the answer via the fastest possible route. He had an unhappy customer on the phone and wanted a quick solution. It was obvious that if this continued, Maria was going to get annoyed enough to snap at the customer support representatives interrupting her. A better response (one that always works in this situation at this company) was to ask the support rep to sit down with her. "Let's work through this together. I think there's a database item on the issue; I'll bring up the system. Let's look it up. Ah, here it is. We'll read it together." It usually takes only one of these responses to convince the support rep that it's now more difficult to* *come to the new project manager for the answer than it is to look up the answer himself. Problem solved with no hard feelings.*

One slightly sideways version of this is that sometimes you have to let things hit the floor (fail) to get them fixed. I would never do this with something that truly endangers the project, and I only do it with a contingency plan in my pocket and ready to go, but sometimes you have to stop covering for people before they will do the right thing. This usually happens when you bail someone out over and over until they depend on you do it in the future.

True Story *A long time ago in a galaxy far, far away, I worked for a large technical start-up. I was working on a very complex software project and found when we got to the final builds that the integrated help component wasn't ready. I was informed that this usually happened with releases and the tech writing group and that the build team typically rebuilt with a sigh and QA had to be delayed (and the QA people worked extra hours to get the releases out on schedule). We went down that path for the first release I was involved in, but you can imagine that QA was not happy to be taking the brunt of the punishment for this particular process, and it did in fact endanger the project for every single release. The division head had no idea this was happening, and I didn't think she needed to hear about it. For the next release I simply informed everyone that the final build would be the final build and let it go from there. The technical writers followed their usual process and expected the rest of the team to accommodate a late delivery. Instead, I turned the project red and let management know we'd have to slip but that we had a contingency plan to rebuild and to delay and compress QA (that is, we would do what was always done). The technical writing team wasn't happy about it, but they never missed another deadline on my projects. The QA and build teams were ecstatic to be able to execute their plans without adjusting every release. We made it easier to do the right thing and deliver on schedule.*

STEP 8

———

BE A TOURIST

Why Do the Other Locations Seem So Disconnected?

So you've established relationships, built your team, and celebrated, but you're still having trouble really connecting all the parts of your team with each other to form a cohesive whole.

Your team might be spread over several different locations—different buildings, different cities, different countries. Virtual teams—ones that keep contact over distances and largely electronically rather than in person—are increasingly common in today's world. (Although truth to tell, when I worked at IBM many years ago lots of teams were already virtual.) The tools to support virtual teams are much more interesting, not to mention useful, than they've ever been before. The stuff that I'm going to talk about here helps keep everyone informed and feeling like an important part of the group no matter where their desk lives or how parts of their personal lives may be different than the majority. People who feel like second-class team citizens are unhappy people, and unhappy people can ruin your beautiful plan. You can make major missteps if you're not paying enough attention to *all* your project team.

Not only do you need to pay attention to what's going on with your project in each of the locations, you need to understand the culture (or even cultures) in each location to avoid costly and sometimes embarrassing mistakes.

There's a label for working effectively across cultures: "cultural intelligence." It's still an emerging field, but it's on the continuum with emotional intelligence and social intelligence, and it's useful even if your whole team is sitting in the same room.

Pretty much every discussion on cultural intelligence illustrates the concept with this: at one time there were posters advertising HSBC at Heathrow Airport in London. The posters showed three identical pictures of a grasshopper. The pictures were in a column. On one grasshopper picture was written "USA—Pest"; on the second, "China—Pet"; and on the third, "Northern Thailand—Appetizer." I don't think I've ever seen a better example of how things can go wrong fast if you aren't prepared with an understanding of cultural differences.

As project managers, we ignore it at our peril (even if we're not eating grasshoppers in China).

There are a few working definitions of cultural intelligence floating around but nothing really easy to get your hands around. In general, cultural intelligence involves recognizing that cultural differences exist, educating yourself on those differences, and being willing not only to continue learning but also to practice cultural customs at the appropriate times.

As you know by now, working with people in ways that are comfortable for them is essential to having a satisfied team. Satisfied teams deliver projects on time and to spec. This includes *all* team members in *all* locations.

Most people think immediately of working with teams in different countries when they talk about cultural intelligence. The big blockers like language are pretty well known, but there are plenty of smaller stumbling blocks to working effectively with those from other cultures. Fortunately, there are plenty of building blocks to keep a virtual team together. Some cultural differences are very subtle (career experience, different companies, different environments), may happen all at one location, and may need some research to uncover.

Different areas of the same country can have pretty significant differences, even though we tend to think in terms of one country, one culture.

True Story *When I work with people from the U.S. South, say Atlanta, I often start a conversation with something other than work. How's the weather, how's your family, something that eases into the work conversation. If I don't do that, the Atlanta folks sometimes see me as rude and abrupt and will be much less likely to put me at the top of their list when I need information. They certainly won't seek out conversations with me because those conversations will be uncomfortable for them. On the other hand, if I do this too often with a client in New York or California they will sometimes think I'm wasting their time. Those clients want to get down to business. In the U.S. Midwest I usually start conversations with something other than work as well, although the need to do so generally isn't quite as pronounced as it often is in the southern United States. It's not a different national culture, but regional culture can be just as important to understand. It's important to note here that I take a middle-of-the-road approach with any individual, no matter where they're located, until I understand how the person likes to work. Stereotypes often exist for a reason, but that's not an excuse to depend on them.*

Another True Story *I work with project managers in Eastern Europe. The main office for one company is in a city in the eastern part of the country and the culture there is very Russian. They think nothing of laughing at someone for making a careless mistake, and no one takes any offense from it. The person who made the mistake laughs too and moves on. From my U.S. perspective interactions sometimes seem abrupt. When this company opened an office on the western side of the same country, the working relationship between the new office and the existing one was strained at first. It turned out that the new office* *was in an area with a more European culture, so that the seeming abruptness affected them as it had me. The moral of the story is that it's not just the United States that has regional culture, so wherever you are and whomever you're working with may not operate in quite the way you expect if you haven't done your homework.*

People from **another company** that you partner with—vendors, resellers, outsourced resources—may come in with different approaches than your own company. Take the time to figure out how they work and how best to work with them and you'll have a better, more productive relationship. This can be really important when you're involved in a merger or joint venture.

True Story *Early in my career I worked for a large global company with strict processes and hierarchies. That company acquired a Silicon Valley company whose motto was "A great place to work." I had friends who had previously left the big company to go to the smaller company and gotten a taste of that small-company culture, and they were not happy with news of the acquisition. They immediately anticipated changes that would transform the culture of their new company. I was part of a large team with members from both companies (but significantly more from the acquiring company) that was supposed to figure out how to merge the various processes and software programs between them. I was really excited to try to bring some of the more progressive processes into my company and looked forward to helping the smaller company get some rigor in the production and warehousing processes they were having some issues with. Unfortunately, I was a very small cog in some very large gears and really didn't have a lot of say in the big picture. Some of us from both companies had a little 5th Wave cartoon on our binders that had two guys in suits furiously arm wrestling and the caption "After the initial merger of two companies comes the delicate process of selecting a dominant software system." In the end, my company was the bigger gorilla and just tried to impose its old-school corporate culture onto this young Silicon Valley company. The "great place to work" employees went elsewhere to find the culture* *they wanted and the whole facility ended up shutting down. It was an object lesson in how ignoring corporate culture can end in disaster.*

Even in your own company there can be **different subcultures**.

One of the really tough ones, especially in the high-tech world, is the collision of employees who are just out of college, are ready to work themselves to death, and make work their number-one life priority (at least for now) with team members who have families and lives outside of work. These can be a little hard to balance within the same team. If you have this culture clash, you'll need to manage it carefully. Don't allow any important decisions to be made outside of working hours unless the entire team is present. Make a habit, and a process, of having people who *think* they've made a decision outside the full team bring that "decision" as a proposal to the full team for consideration and discussion. Don't reward hours spent; reward results. Don't associate proximity with hours working, either—people with families often work from home late into the night. As a plus, you'll have a more balanced team, and those with more experience are weighing in visibly to all the decisions no matter who proposes them.

I have a few global company stories plus one from a California start-up that illustrate culture wars.

True Story *The California start-up had bought companies in the United Kingdom (two of them) and Canada. Everyone had to work together to get the product out the door. It was a really complex software product and the atmosphere sometimes got a little tense. When I arrived, I was fresh from a very hierarchical company, and because of that experience was able to see one of the major sources of tension that others more involved in the situation were missing. In the UK, there was extreme loyalty to one's manager. Even if someone there disagreed with their manager they just repeated the manager's position and expected the person in the United States with an issue to escalate to management. At that point it was management's job to make a decision.*

In the United States, however, the environment was very open to technical opinions and arguments from anyone, regardless of position in the company hierarchy. Escalation to management was considered an option of last resort, to be taken when you had absolutely failed to come to a conclusion, and as such was considered something of an insult. You can imagine what was happening. The U.S. employees were upset because the UK employees went over their heads without trying to work things out. The UK employees were upset because the U.S. employees kept nagging them about things they couldn't change instead of escalating. Without the outside look that I was able to bring, it was really difficult for anyone in the middle of it all to see what was happening. The understanding of the two different cultures helped us get past a fair amount of the buildup of tension.

Another True Story When I worked for a big corporation, at one point I supported the accounting group. There was concern because several people in the Research group (a large group that occupied a whole building) didn't seem to have cashed their paychecks (in the way-back days of paper checks). Someone went physically to the building to investigate (the researchers never answered their phones or email) and found that several research scientists had been stuffing their checks in their desks so they could get back to work. I think that probably started a big initiative for automatic deposit, which was in its infancy. The accountants really could not get their heads around this viewpoint, but the research scientists were very connected to and excited by their work. Two incredibly different cultures collided in the same company at the same address.

Yet Another True Story When I first started with IBM and had a trip scheduled to the East Coast, I was told that you could always tell when someone was at HQ from west of the Mississippi, because they wore a brown suit. It was pretty clear that you needed to wear black, gray, or navy blue if you were presenting to someone on the East Coast. (I once was required to present my badge at an education building because, although I was wearing a conservative gray suit with a purple *silk blouse and sensible [if high-heeled] gray pumps, I had the audacity to wear purple nylons. The receptionist couldn't believe that I actually worked at IBM and wore purple stockings. I was a cultural anomaly.)*

One More True Story *At one international company it was well known (and people were pretty envious) that the cafeterias and vending machines in Germany had beer and in France had wine. The same company in the United States was very much a teetotal organization, so this was a very visible nod to the culture of the countries where the company was operating.*

For differences within your own company, you'll just have to research and rely on word of mouth, but for corporate cultures writ large you can check out Tettra's Culture Codes. This website has the culture decks for many companies (https://tettra.co/culture-codes /culture-decks/). Bear in mind that these are the stated cultures of the companies, so your mileage may vary with actual experience.

If **someone has recently moved** to your team from another country, area, or company, pay attention. They may have difficulty adjusting or fitting in, which can be really demoralizing. Give them a chance to tell you how things are different, what they like about your team, what they don't like about your team's operations, and what they like from their previous location. Do it in private, and let them know what might be good to bring to the team, what you don't think will work, and what might cause trouble. One of the biggest problems you can have with someone coming into your team is a constant "We did it better in my other team/company/location" attitude. Facing that kind of attitude, even practices that would be better if adopted by your team will meet resistance. Work to manage it, and you'll have a happy team and find some ways to improve at the same time.

People come to your project with **different levels of education and experience**. This can make a difference in viewpoint in some cases, but your bigger problem may be in vocabulary. It's not that people with more education necessarily have a bigger vocabulary, but they've by definition been in at least one environment where exercising that vocabulary is encouraged and rewarded. In a less rarified environment, that can be intimidating or seen as condescending. It's hard to manage: you don't want anyone dumbing down their language thinking that others don't understand (they do, they just think it's stuck-up). The best way I've found to manage it is to have anyone who likes to use a lot of big or unusual words address it with other members of the team. It can be in a meeting, but one-on-one is usually easier, and word will get around. (If on the other hand you have someone who really does use language as a weapon, you'll want to take them aside and get them to knock it off, or you'll have a mutiny on your hands.)

Different religions are nothing new, but it's important to be aware of some of the requirements of various religions. You can't ask people what religion they follow, but you can be open to religious holidays or customs important to people on your team and have a plan for accommodating them. If there are religious customs that some team members must follow, know what those are and provide for them. If you've done your homework and established relationships with the members of your team, they will feel comfortable letting you know what they need.

Different languages or accents are much more common now than they used to be, even in the same office. Be aware that some people may have an initial difficulty understanding accents they haven't encountered before and be sure to slow down meetings and check that everyone understands what's been said. If you see puzzled looks on faces, step in and ask the speaker to repeat herself.

Finally, there's a lot of cultural (and subcultural) variation in **what people wear**. There are the obvious ones (head coverings, dresses, shoe types, etc.) and the more subtle ones (piercings, makeup, etc.). Unless someone's manner of dress violates a clear code (bare feet, for example, are against health codes in many environments), treat manner of dress as a personal choice. If the clothing seems to be cultural and you're comfortable with the person sporting it, feel free to ask about it. Otherwise, it's worth the time for a quick internet search to learn more. That doesn't mean you need to (or should) comment, but more knowledge is always better. And compliments are usually welcome.

So how do you manage all this?

From a cultural intelligence perspective, three facets are commonly referred to: Head, Hands, and Heart.

Head is the intellectual part of the equation. It isn't just the research part, although that will help. You'll get some information about how to operate. The reference is more about having a plan to learn. Go in ready to observe. Have your questions ready and keep an open mind. If there's something specific you're worried about or need to know about, have a strategy for learning about it. A lot of learning is going to take place when you're interacting with people from other cultures, whatever and wherever they are, and you need to be in a position to take advantage of it.

Hands is about the physical part. Knowing is not the same as doing or acting. In some cultures it's rude to smile openly; knowing that is not enough. You need to cover your mouth when you smile (or do whatever else might be appropriate). Knowing that you hand your business cards to a Japanese colleague with both hands and turned so she can read it is not enough. You need to hand over your cards that way to that person. You may not do it perfectly the first time, but here is where the Head part comes in. Watch how the other person does it and work to get it right. People are usually patient and encouraging if they know you're trying.

Heart is not at all what you're thinking. The heart part of cultural intelligence is your confidence in yourself. You need to believe that you can learn about other cultures and be proficient in it.

So there's the theory. But let's get to some practical implementation of that theory.

Identify likely areas of difference. It's better to be forewarned and forearmed. Identify the likely cultural differences on your team, including your extended team, so you can take the next step.

TRY IT

Identify cultural differences on your own team:

- From another country
- From another company
- Recently moved
- Different education level
- Different religion
- Different language/accent
- Different clothing

RESEARCH

There's no substitute for doing your homework. Start with the internet. Two good sources for country culture information are cyborlink.com (for international customs) and Todaytranslations.com (for Australian, UK, and Brazilian business customs). If you know someone familiar with (or better yet, from or part of) the culture you'll be working with, talk to him. This is especially effective if he's been in both cultures because it's easier for him to understand and explain the differences. After the basic research, it's usually okay to just ask people about their customs and what behavior is appropriate, particularly if you've established a contact at another location who has given you background.

GO FOR IT

This is where the Heart comes in. If you're worried you'll offend, try things out on an individual in private before you try in a group setting, but don't hang back because you're afraid. The consequences of failing to act are far greater than the consequences of not getting it quite right the first time.

True Story *Every time I went to Romania I studied Romanian language tapes. I started at home and continued while traveling so I was as current with them as I could be. Most of my Romanian counterparts were initially mystified by this—after all, everyone I was working with directly spoke excellent English. (In fact, pretty much everyone I encountered, from taxi drivers to store clerks, spoke multiple languages, although English wasn't always one of them.) But the effort (even when people laughed at my pronunciation or the idioms I learned from the tapes) was worth it. I was trying—visibly—and learning a lot in the process. (One time when I got there the only taxi driver at two in the morning spoke French but not English. I did my best in Romanian after 22 hours of travel and a lot longer with no sleep, he corrected my pronunciation,*

I got a lot of information about the landmarks we were passing, and I had a lot of fun.)

OBSERVE

You can learn a lot from watching people. It's pretty obvious that you can learn about customs from observation, but you need to go one better to integrate your social intelligence with the cultural intelligence. Notice when people are uncomfortable with differences, so you can get more information about what they're uncomfortable with and share that information with the rest of the team. Know when someone's discomfort means they need different methods. Read body language when you can. This isn't an exact science, but it's usually pretty clear when someone is defensive, trying not to be noticed, or looking for an escape route.

SHARE

Don't keep your newfound knowledge to yourself. Educate your team members. If they're comfortable, have people from different cultural backgrounds talk a bit about their culture in a safe environment. (Bring food—see Step 9. You could even try some of that culture's food.)

DEALING WITH MULTIPLE LOCATIONS

Different locations present issues beyond cultural differences. Time differences, the inability to read people, and feelings of isolation all come into play.

My first tip is to have a **key contact**, an inside man at each location. That person can be your eyes and ears and let you know how people are feeling about the project and the team. That's not to say you need a spy. You just need feet on the ground to catch those subtle clues that you can't pick up on from a distance.

Next, set up as much **face-to-face communication** as you can between the teams. Travel is great when it's possible. Videoconferencing is next best, and it's easier now than it's ever been. Phone conferences are better than nothing, but without being able to see individuals you can't read expressions, and sometimes you can't even tell who's speaking. Remember that Vice President of Engineering who swore that the half-life of face-to-face communication is six months? That theory proved out many times. There are rarely email flame wars between teams who have to look at each other regularly.

Use **instant message groups** whenever possible—Skype, Slack, even text messaging. When you do this, people can keep more regular hours and know that when they go to work in the morning they'll be able to check the group and see what's happened while they were asleep. Everyone stays informed, and everyone's opinion is expressed and considered.

The **team web pages** can be especially important here (see Step 6). Pictures of everyone, hobbies, and background are great ways for team members in different locations to feel connected. Pictures of the different offices will help everyone understand the different environments (for example, if one location has an open office plan and another location has individual offices, those in the open office may be less comfortable being as straightforward in discussions unless they're in a conference room with a door than those in individual offices will be). Post project information on these web pages, too, so that everyone has instant and equal access to documents, status, meeting notes, and any other happenings. When you do team-building exercises at one location, be sure to post pictures to the website so everyone can join in the fun.

If you have groups at several locations in the same general area, **have meetings in different buildings**, different floors, and different rooms so everyone has something at a team level happening in their area. Encourage people to walk to the other area instead of just calling and emailing all the time. (You'll need to model this behavior, and you can get someone who sits near you and take them along to get things going.)

Although it can be a little more difficult, consider **scheduling regular full-team meetings at different times** so that every time zone has meetings during reasonable working hours at least some of the time. It makes everyone more understanding of the time differences and puts everyone on an equal footing (at least with respect to discomfort!).

If you're giving out **prizes, awards, or tchotchkes,** be sure they go to all the locations. With your contact in each location, you should be able to get the items ordered and available everywhere at the same time.

When handing out **key assignments,** be sure to give some to every location (as appropriate of course). It can be a big temptation to keep the most important tasks close to you, as the project manager, so you can monitor them, but that sets up a perception that your location is the important one.

A NOTE ON THE LINE BETWEEN CULTURAL DIFFERENCES AND DISCRIMINATION

Some differences in viewpoint and approach may be part of a culture or subculture, but their expression cannot be tolerated, either from a human or a legal standpoint. You know which ones these are—things like gender, religion, and race. Address specifics with individuals in private, and get your HR organization engaged when necessary, but don't allow these differences to be displayed in a team environment. Call bad behavior out of bounds, quote company policy, or do whatever you need to do when it occurs, but stop the behavior immediately. If it continues in a team environment, you may need to stop whatever is going on (probably a meeting or call) and take the offender aside to deal with it immediately. Allowing it to continue will not only damage your team, possibly irreparably; it will put both you and the company in legal jeopardy.

———

FEED YOUR TEAM

The Magic of Chocolate, the Utility of Pizza, and the Universal Language of Food

Why talk about food in a book about project management and social intelligence? Every being on the planet has a personal relationship with food. More than just fuel, we use food as a way to communicate across boundaries. Think about the nonhumans I've mentioned in this book—horses, dogs, and cats all trust the people who bring them food. Cats may take a little longer to win trust with food, but win it you will if you're consistent and provide it without demand. People are a lot more subtle about it, but we can still use food as an aid to help us establish and maintain relationships on an individual level and among team members.

True Story *In the same reorganization that moved me from Engineering Director to VP of Technical Services, the Silicon Valley company I worked for bought a company in Eastern Europe and transferred Engineering to the purchased company. The former CEO of the Eastern European company (we'll call him Peter) thus became the VP of Engineering for the Silicon Valley company. In this capacity, Peter traveled often to Silicon Valley, spreading chaos and unrest as he went. Peter had conflicting feelings about working with me: on one hand, I was a woman—clearly inferior to him and all other males because of my gender—on the other hand, I was a Vice President (he was very impressed with titles and hierarchy) and had two Engineering degrees.*

I had no such conflicting feelings about working with Peter (since I not only had to deal with him directly but also had to either rescue or restrain various women in my organization whenever they came into contact with him). The absolute best outcome of any of our meetings was an impasse. Until the day Peter asked me to meet with him over breakfast. There I met a completely different Peter—courteous, forthcoming, willing to discuss and compromise. After that meeting, we had all our working sessions at restaurants over breakfast, lunch, or dinner. We never did agree on anything in the office, as the restaurant version Peter never showed up there, but we were able to get work done as long as we were meeting over a meal.

I spent a lot of time trying to figure out what was different about leaving the office. At first I thought maybe the privacy of being off-site was the key, but it was a lot less private in restaurants than it was in my office or a conference room at work. Eventually, it became clear that it was the addition of food that was working the magic.

This turns out to be true in general. Unless we're worried about poison, meals are a safe place to gather. Weapons are not allowed, people remove their armor (both literally and figuratively), and there are cultural rules and mores about appropriate behavior during meals.

Most of what I'll tell you in this step I discovered more or less by accident. I never sat down and thought, "What could I do with food?" A great deal of it came about while trying to reduce stress for my team. I eventually put it all together (and in a few cases found research that supported my own experiential findings) as I was coaching new project managers and making suggestions that had to do with food. All that is to say that my findings aren't strictly scientific. There's very little available research in the area that I've been able to find in periodic searches, but my experience has been very consistent.

Think of all the customs and values wrapped up in meals celebrating events—everything from Thanksgiving turkey in the United

States to Twelfth Night cakes in the United Kingdom. Rituals around Shabbat, toasts at weddings—there are food-related activities in every culture. It's no accident that studies show that children who have dinner with the family at least three nights a week fare better in school, have fewer medical problems, and have fewer behavioral issues.[1]

What does this have to do with project management, you ask? Good question. It points the way for us to use food to help foster and maintain relationships with and among team members. Want to establish that relationship with the new team member? Have lunch with her. Studies show not just that people bond faster over meals but that they bond faster when eating the *same* food.[2] So when you take that new team member out to lunch, have her order first. If you like what she's having, order the same thing. Who knew?

BLACK GOLD

True Story *When I was a first-time manager, my grandfather sent me a box of candy he got from the old-fashioned candy store in his town— every single month. I couldn't handle that much candy, so I took it to work and put it in a bowl for other people to help share the weight gain. People seemed to enjoy it, so that became my custom. Eventually, the candy store went out of business and the packages stopped, but people were still coming to my office looking for candy. It was around Halloween time when the candy deliveries ceased, so I put some Halloween candy into the bowl—chocolate candy—and that led me to the discovery of the black gold of project management: chocolate. Eventually, I found other project managers who had stumbled on the same truth.*

If you keep a bowl of chocolate in your office, people will stop by to have some. This turns out to be a valuable tool in a number of ways:

- The more stress people are under, the faster the chocolate goes away. You can judge the state of your project by the speed at which the chocolate disappears—the faster it goes, the more risky your project. (I've had parts of projects where I went through two to three bags of chocolate *a day*.)

- Because of the actual benefits of chocolate vis-à-vis stress relief,[3] you're helping your team just that little bit more. (By the time this study came out, my fellow project managers and I had to laugh at the need for an actual extensive study to come to this conclusion.)

- I learned the concept of reciprocation in management psychology—that human beings are hard wired to reciprocate favors so as not to be in debt. In general I find that people reciprocate my chocolate provision with information. I couldn't ask for a better payment. I typically stock my bowl with Hershey's Kisses; individually wrapped chocolates means that people tend to stand in my office while unwrapping the chocolate and deciding whether to take another one, telling me what's on their minds as they do this.

- I have had situations where people run into my office, grab a handful of chocolate, and run off. That's generally not good news, but at least I know they're in trouble.

SNACKS

Snacks are a great way to surprise your team when they're working hard and need an energy boost.

You can also use some kinds of snacks, like popcorn, to lure people out of their offices to take a bit of a break and talk. Communication is always good. (Don't burn the popcorn in the microwave though; no one will ever forget it if you do.)

More than that, snacks are the perfect way to get people to a meeting on time, especially if it's an early morning meeting. Snacks will also help get people through a multihour meeting (no matter how interesting the topic, energy and attention will lapse after a while).

Beware of bringing snacks to a recurring meeting, though; once you bring them, people will expect them at every meeting. Decide if it's worth bringing snacks to every recurring meeting before you start.

Some important rules for snacks:

- Find out people's food preferences and issues. If you have someone who is on a strict diet, be sure to bring something they can eat. (If you bring donuts, also bring some fruit, for example.)
- Don't bring messy foods—no one wants to sit through a two-hour meeting with a banana peel in front of them or a peach pit on the table.
- Don't bring too many different types of food at once, or people will spend their time deciding on food instead of paying attention to the meeting.
- Bring napkins (and plates if necessary).
- If you bring something with a lot of sugar, plan a break after an hour or so or you'll have people falling asleep.

Best bets: I find that grapes, cleaned strawberries, donuts, and bagels all work well for meetings. Be sure drinks are available, even if that's only water in a pitcher on the table (but in that case be sure there are cups!).

LUNCHES

Bringing in lunch for your team is a nice plus. I've worked at Silicon Valley companies where not only lunch but also dinner is provided regularly, but that tends to suggest that people should be working a whole lot of hours, and it's a bit less common than it used to be.

You can use lunch either to keep people working comfortably and allow them to get out of the office at a reasonable hour during crunch time or to get people to take a break and communicate. There are different rules for each.

General rules:

- As with snacks, know people's likes and restrictions. There's not much that's more demoralizing than to show up for a team lunch and have nothing there that you can eat.
- Don't get anything too messy—no one wants to go through the day wearing part of their lunch.
- The basics will go fast, no matter how much people protest that they won't. I can't count the number of times I've said, "Order pepperoni," for a pizza lunch, gotten a general response of "That's boring, no one wants it," and then arrived a few minutes late to find every piece of the one pepperoni pizza gone. With prepackaged lunches, I had a friend who would always order a peanut butter and jelly sandwich and someone would always take it (even though everyone knew what they themselves had ordered) before he got to the room. Never underestimate the value of comfort food!

If you want people to **stay and talk**, avoid buffets and prepackaged lunches. People will grab those and head out. I've found that pizza is perfect for getting people to stay and talk. No one wants to load up a plate with four slices of different pizzas, so they'll try one at a time and hang out and talk. Food like dim sum and tapas can work for this also.

If you want people to **grab and go**, prepackaged meals like sandwiches or preordered lunches are great. Buffets work too—people seem to see buffets as an invitation to load up and head out.

DINNERS

If you're in crunch time and working late is unavoidable for the team, ordering in dinner is a nice sign of appreciation. Buffets with a good selection are the best choice for bringing in dinner because people can pick what they like and come back for more later.

Dinners for special occasions are more about celebrating and marking milestones, which we discussed in Step 6. *Never* have a dinner to mark a special occasion actually held in the workplace. It just doesn't send the right message.

ALCOHOL

I highly recommend avoiding alcoholic beverages for work situations unless you're operating in a culture in which alcohol is common at all meals and for all people. Even then I recommend weighing possible benefits against the plethora of minefields. Some people simply do not drink alcoholic beverages, which immediately sets up a divide. Some people don't handle it well, which does not bode well for your team. It's an unnecessary risk for very little reward.

FOOD AND CULTURAL INTELLIGENCE

Food can be a great opening to learning about a particular culture. In some areas it's harder than others, but in most urban areas you can find at least one restaurant serving cuisine from almost any culture. Eating that food, asking about its source and preparation, and learning about its history and place in the culture can open the door to more cultural sharing.

True Story *At one start-up several of the engineers had tried (well, tried lots of times) Ethiopian food. Naturally, the rest of us wanted to try it too, and they took us in groups to one of the two local Ethiopian restaurants and explained the food as best they could. There weren't any Ethiopians on our team, so we weren't learning team culture, but it gave us an opening to have one of the restaurants cater a company event or two. The owners of the restaurant would bring the food and set it up. By that time they knew us and would answer all kinds of questions about the food itself and Ethiopian culture. Not only did we learn a lot about it, it was another team experience to share.*

Another True Story *At one company in Silicon Valley there were a number of people from Vietnam in our group. They went out regularly for Vietnamese food at local restaurants and invited me. (Once I tried it, I was hooked; I love Vietnamese food.) It was an education. There were a lot of procedures—separate dishes, what to roll in rice paper, putting greens into soup and eating it with chopsticks. I got an excellent education in Vietnamese basics—that dessert is mainly in drinks because of the heat, that there are two different distinct cuisines (French-influenced vs. Chinese-influenced) and how they differed, how the French influence brought about use of a European alphabet. It was fascinating, I learned a lot, and it was a great experience with team members. I also had to do the hands part of Cultural Intelligence—for example, the spring rolls the Vietnamese and Chinese members of our little party made looked very different from my sloppy burrito-like ones (mine took a lot longer to make too), but I tried and laughed at my efforts along with everyone else.*

Yet Another True Story *The first day I worked at a company as an intern, a large group of people from the team went to a local Chinese restaurant. I'd had Chinese food exactly once in my life (rural Pennsylvania was a little short on Chinese restaurants) and had never used chopsticks.*

This restaurant only had chopsticks, so I had to learn in a hurry. One of the American members of our party gave me instructions and demonstrated, at which time another new employee who was originally from China started to giggle. The American asked the new employee if he was doing it wrong, and she told him that he was doing it exactly right—the way her parents always tried to get her to do it (but that she held her chopsticks "wrong"). I'll never know if I would have had the courage to try chopsticks in that environment at that point in my life, but with no other option I dove in. It was a lesson all around and a really nice way to be part of the team right away. As a side note, my friend, Eileen, who taught me to nag (but more on that later), gave me several sets of chopsticks to practice with a few years later. Once I learned to eat macaroni salad with them, anything was possible. The moral of that story is to practice whatever and wherever you can, even if it's hard at first.

TRY IT

Give it a try—match the occasion or need in the first column to the food in the second column. Do you know why each food choice is (or is not) the best choice for each occasion?

OCCASION

A. Lunch meeting
   (discussion and mingling)
B. Grab and work at your desk
C. Morning meeting where
   people keep coming in late
D. Take a break and talk a bit
E. Work-through-lunch meeting
F. Midafternoon-slump meeting

FOOD

1. Buffet
   (maybe a theme buffet)
2. Donuts and grapes
3. Pizza
4. Sandwiches
5. Cheese and crackers
6. Popcorn

ANSWER

A—3: In a meeting or just in a room, pizza encourages people to talk. Your meeting will be a little less formal as people move around, but they'll relax and communicate.

B—4: Sandwiches are easy for people to pick up and eat at their desk. There's not a lot of mess or a lot of leftovers that will leave a smell, which is a plus for eating in an office.

C—2: People love donuts and will show up to get their first choice. Grapes are a nice alternative for anyone not wanting to eat the high-calorie choice (be sure to get seedless grapes).

D—6: Nothing draws people like the smell of fresh popcorn.

E—1: People are happy to get their lunches from a buffet and carry them somewhere else. It's fun if you can add a theme and let people know ahead of time, but not necessary.

F—5: Avoid sugar for a midafternoon meeting. People are already slumping from lunch; cheese and crackers fix that problem.

STEP 10

WALK THE LINE

People, Process, and the Fine Art of Nagging

Now you're fully prepared to deal with your team members with emotional intelligence, with your whole team with social and cultural intelligence, and with other teams with all three. You know how to communicate, how to motivate, how to celebrate, and how to eat.

That's only part of the whole project management equation, though. There's no doubt that this emotional intelligence stuff is crucial—without people, there's no way to build a product, and without emotional and social intelligence you lose the people. The whole reason you have a team, though, is to complete a project. Without the project, the people have no jobs and the team has no reason for being. And without some process, the people on the team are missing the organization they need to produce the product. All three pieces are vitally important to the success of the project— people, product (the result of the project), and process. You're there to provide the balance. Project managers wear many hats, and we have to change them at, well, the drop of a hat.

An important thing to remember is that the process is there to serve the business, not the opposite. All that lovely process goes to waste if you can't make a product with it. Bringing process to the table requires flexibility. If any of the processes aren't working for your project or your team, you will need to adjust. Here's a place where people and process intersect. If a standard process isn't working for your project, you'll need to make changes. Bring your team into the discussion and see what changes they feel are necessary for the team to operate at their peak—the place where the process supports them. If there are standard processes that are working well there's no need to change them (sometimes teams get a little giddy if they think they can change processes at will). Standard processes are standard for a reason, and organizations tend to resist deviation from them, so if you do need to make an adjustment, be sure to cover yourself adequately. Document why the change is needed, what the change is, and how you'll still meet the requirements of the process. If someone or some organization needs to approve the change, definitely get the approval, but remember that the someone is a person, and use your new cat-herding skills to approach the person in a way that is non-threatening. (For example, marching in and dropping a change on someone's desk probably won't get the response you're hoping for. Be prepared to explain and thank the person for their support.)

You need to be open to explaining your actions—to your team, to your management, and to outside organizations that might question your processes or decisions. (If you can't explain a decision you made, that's a hint that it might not have been a good one.) Your team members aren't children, and "because I said so" is not going to work, tempting as that may be. Sometimes you have no choice—there's a mandated decision or process that you and your team have to follow. Be transparent about that. There are ways to document concerns with mandates and decisions that we'll get into later, but full disclosure with your team is (almost) always the best policy.

GOALS

While we're on the topic of clarity, let's talk some more about goals. Your project has goals and your team needs to know what they are. If your project was created with the goals in place before the team is created, discuss the goals with the team. Be sure that everyone understands the project goals and is on board for them. Check to see that each person on the team knows how she will contribute to each of the goals. (If you can't see how each person will contribute, maybe your team makeup isn't quite right. Everyone should have a place and a contribution.)

You can use a 4 dials exercise as a framework to discuss project goals. The dials on a project can be adjusted, but they're all important: Content, Schedule, Cost, and Quality. Your project should have goals for each of these. (In practice, Agile software projects often have variable content, but there's usually a base requirement even there.) In actual practice, my experience has been that two of the dials can be "pegged"—set without allowing for any change—and two of them are likely to have to change sometime during the project whether you pick them or not. You and your team should understand which of the dials are unmovable and which can be changed (always with backup documentation and, if necessary, approval). That sets a guideline for the team during the project. Having a common understanding will help each of the team members make good decisions on small everyday issues, contributing to both the motivation (trust, knowledge, ability to make decisions) and team interactions (everyone has the same understanding, so can use that as a basis for discussion when there's a disagreement).

The goals and the status of each one should be a regular review item. We tend to do these reviews with our clients or management periodically, but it's at least as important that the team review the progress toward the goals very regularly. Put the goals and their status front and center in team meetings so that if someone sees a danger, the whole team can understand what it is and work to get back on track—together. It will also help everyone involved understand if the dials have changed and make a course correction. Everyone is at least marching in the same direction even if they have different drummers.

To add to the complexity of the people side, the individuals on the team will have their own personal goals. It's up to you to understand what they are, so that relationship you've established will come in handy. Some goals are probably going to be documented and therefore easy to articulate, others may be a little harder to nail down. Wherever possible, support the individuals' goals within the project goals.

True Story *I had an engineer who desperately wanted to go into marketing. I thought that it might not be a good fit, but he was pretty determined. Instead of either telling him no (which would just leave me with a frustrated engineer working on marketing in spite of me) or just sponsoring a move into a position where I thought he might not be happy or successful, I let him work with the marketing department for a project on which he was an engineer. He was the official liaison with the marketing department (while still doing the necessary engineering on the project), which got him a good view into what the marketing jobs were about as well as giving him some visibility to the marketing folks. The marketing folks loved having someone technical available to them, and he got to see that he was not going to be happy doing what they were doing. The project profited with an excellent engineering-marketing relationship, the team member profited by being able to look before he leapt, and my department profited by keeping a talented engineer.*

Another True Story *In another company in another galaxy, I had the same situation. (I'm not sure what it is that drives engineers to want to go into marketing. It must be the glamour of it all.) I used a similar strategy, letting the engineer perform a liaison function with the marketing department while doing her engineering work on the project. This time it worked differently. She absolutely loved the marketing work, and the marketing people were impressed with her approach and* *ideas. We put together a development plan so that by the end of the project she'd be in a good position to transition to a job in marketing. Once again everyone came out ahead. The project profited with the marketing-engineering relationship and the fresh approach and ideas the engineer brought, the engineer profited by getting some marketing experience and making herself known in the marketing group, and the company profited by gaining a new and talented marketing person. (I, of course, lost a key engineer, but sometimes you have to take one for the team.)*

A MATCHING GAME AND A BALANCING ACT

At its heart, project management is both a matching game and a balancing act.

You need to match people to roles, using both hard and soft skills as well as priorities and talent scarcity, to keep everyone happy and the project on track. You need to match people with their learning styles so you can communicate effectively. You need to try to match personal goals to project goals whenever possible so that everyone comes out ahead. Finally, you need to match people with motivators so that work on your project moves along and no one is dragging or looking for another position.

The balance is even more complex than the match game. You need to balance people with other people, not favoring one over others and helping them get along. You need to balance the needs of the project with the needs of the people, and both of those need to support the product of the project. You need to not only match individual goals with project goals, you need to balance fulfilling personal goals with the overriding need to meet the project goals.

Perhaps most important from an emotional and social intelligence perspective, you have to balance immediate progress with sustained improvement or production. In some ways, this often equates to the carrot and stick issue. Sometimes you require immediate progress—to meet a milestone, because you're behind, or because the situation has changed. The stick in that case is usually overtime (and the likely results if the overtime doesn't materialize). That's okay once in a while, but you won't be able to use it very often for a number of reasons. My own experience over the years is that, after about two weeks of 60-plus hours all those extra hours start being used to fix problems that have been introduced because people are tired and burned out by working 60-hour weeks. It ends up being a net loss because you have an exhausted team at the end of it and performance degrades even further. If overtime is all the time, or perceived as being required, resentment will be rampant on your team. People will be unmotivated and will probably start looking elsewhere for work—and you won't be able to replace them because you and your project will have a reputation of constant unrewarded overtime. So use it only when you need it, and be sure that everyone on the team is aware of why it's needed and that it will be a short-term situation. Try to adjust future dates to give people a break when you meet the milestone or goal. In horse terms, where carrot and stick originated, horses who are motivated with punishment become resentful, fearful, and sometimes even unmanageable. On the other hand, horses (who are in general extremely food motivated and who often have quite a sweet tooth) will do a lot for a carrot. The carrot is then associated with the activity and eventually becomes unnecessary. The carrot in a project can be just about anything that qualifies as a reward—a team break, time off, a party, a bonus, anything to look forward to at the end. Sustained improvement generally comes with enough of an upside that the improvement itself can be used as a motivator if you're really clear about what that kind of improvement will buy people. If a process can be improved, it might help avoid overtime, produce a better product, enhance the reputation of the team and the people on it, gain recognition for productivity, and even result in promotions or raises. It's up to you to help produce the carrots—be a cheerleader for your team. Be sure that their efforts are recognized both within the team and outside the team, particularly by management and clients.

NAGGING

Project managers nag. It can be frustrating. We all think that people should just do their jobs, but we have to just get over it. Nagging, aka judicious reminders and checking, is part of the job. Our priorities aren't necessarily other people's priorities, so we have to find ways to put our priorities at the top of the list. Nagging is a good way to accomplish that, but you have to do it right in order for it to work. Having people run when they see you coming isn't going to get your project done on time.

The first thing you need to nag effectively is to understand each person's learning style and be sure to use that communication channel whenever possible. Having them actually pick up your communication is the first step to getting a person to complete a task. (If they're sending your emails directly to a folder or your calls directly to voicemail, you're doing it wrong.)

Be nice. If you call someone every day and you're a jerk about it, she is going to feel entirely justified in putting you off. If you call someone every day and you're nice about it, he's not going to have anything to push back against. This does seem to go against common opinion, but I can tell you from personal experience that this is what works.

Give people enough time. If something is due tomorrow and you call this afternoon asking how it's going, you haven't given them enough time to react and get you what you need. The more you work with someone, the better you'll understand how early you need to start to check on deliverables and how often you're going to need to check back.

Finally, be persistent. Call every day if you need to. Use different communication channels until you find the one (or ones) that work. Set yourself reminders to remind people so you don't forget or let it go until too late (yes, it's true, you even have to nag yourself).

True Story *When I was a young and inexperienced project manager, I had a friend, Eileen (yes, the very one who gave me the chopsticks), who also managed projects in my group. When she needed anything from me, she'd call me every single day about it. I'd pick up the phone and hear, "Ms. Wasson, good morning. How are you coming with that thing I need? Not ready yet? Okay, thanks, I'll call back tomorrow." Pretty soon Eileen was at the top of my list because I knew she would call me and ask cheerfully about what I had promised. Every. Single. Day. As it turned out, Eileen was at the top of everyone's list for exactly this reason. She sat near me but didn't come into my office; she could see when I got in and sat down. It was a lesson I never forgot.*

MANAGING YOUR BOSS

Bosses aren't omniscient. If a manager knows every single thing happening with every person in her group, chances are that she's a micromanager and everyone resents her for her lack of trust. Trust, evidenced by lack of micromanaging, works both ways. You can't expect your manager to know what's going on if you don't tell her, so keep her informed.

When I was a manager I had one cardinal rule: no surprises. (I actually wrote this into everyone's performance plan.) As a project manager I have the same rule, and you should always consider it a given. Never put your boss in the position of walking into a meeting with her peers or her manager and being surprised by being asked about something that went wrong. Figure out the easiest way for both of you to keep your boss informed about progress, potential issues, problems with other groups, and things that have gone swimmingly. This doesn't mean that you run to your boss with every little thing. Put it together as a normal means of communication, but make exceptions if there are issues that she needs to know about (or, gods forbid, that she'll otherwise be ambushed about). (If you're having trouble with this, give your manager this book, and maybe she'll set up a weekly meeting with you!)

You also need to manage up. Keep your boss out of your team members' hair. Provide enough information and exposure to let your boss and your team keep some distance from each other while still giving your team members the recognition they deserve and your boss the information she needs.

Spend some time with your boss so you know her expectations of both you and your team. How much authority do you have? When does she want you to escalate? The more you agree on the ground rules, the better your relationship will be. A good relationship with your boss is as important as a good relationship with your team members. Your boss is your support structure in the same way that you support your team. You're also representing your team and its members to your boss. You need to be able to report personnel issues without blacklisting anyone, and you need to represent excellent performance on a regular basis.

Always remember that your boss is dealing with political issues (and sometimes other issues and restrictions) that you may not be aware of. (Any organization with more than one department or more than one project is going to have some kind of politics going on. In general, be happy if most of the politics are above your pay grade.) There are going to be triggers that your manager needs to cover (things that make her own boss crazy), so be sure to ask if there's anything specific she needs information about. It's as hard for your boss to know what you're thinking about as it is for you to know what your team members are thinking about or what they've heard—it requires communication.

Another important rule is to never drop problems in your boss's lap. If there's an issue, never do a drive-by and ask your boss to solve the problem. Communicate the same way you'd like team members to communicate with you. First, be clear about the issue and its relative importance. Second, outline the options you're considering, including their pros and cons. Finally, make a recommendation, and don't be offended if your boss chooses another option, because she may have information you don't. Sometimes you're legitimately stumped—you don't know which option to choose—and it's fine in those cases not to make a recommendation. Assuming you've worked with your team on the issue or it's a personnel issue, after you tell your boss about the issue and its importance, let her know what you've already tried (or what you've considered and discarded). All of this will get you faster resolution to your issues and help maintain your relationship with your manager.

True Story *I worked with a project manager, Bob, who (like most of us) had to prepare an extensive weekly report for his management chain. This report included information from groups and projects other than his own because he was acting as a program manager for a large group. Because it was for an extended group, Bob often needed a particular director's input to ensure the report was accurate. Time after time Bob would try to get that input, but there was a weekly deadline for submitting the report that he couldn't miss so eventually he'd have to submit what he had. As a result the report was sometimes inaccurate, which made it less useful to his management chain and resulted in corrections and time wasted. Bob and I did a retrospective of the process he used to get the director's input (sometimes it helps to get a third party's opinion). He typically sent the report to the director attached to an email that had Bob's specific questions. Sometimes he printed out the report and left it on the director's desk. The few times Bob was* *able to get the information he needed, he had scheduled a meeting with the director to walk through the questions. He had attempted to schedule a weekly meeting, but the director was so busy that it was usually canceled. We went through all this in the usual way—what went right, what didn't go well, what could be improved. Looking at the pattern, I asked if maybe the director was an auditory learner, and as busy as this particular director was, it was likely that she was putting reading reports and emails lower on the list, so that when she got to them it was too late to fix the report. I could almost see the light bulb go on, and Bob had a process improvement to try. From that time on (although he did keep the weekly meeting because face to face worked well on the rare occasions it actually happened), he asked his questions in a voicemail. The response rate improved dramatically, the report was usually accurate, the director didn't feel nagged . . . all in all, a successful personal process improvement based on emotional intelligence.*

USING RISK ANALYSIS TO DISAGREE

You won't always agree with decisions and direction you get from your boss (or her boss even). If you have a great strong relationship you can talk about why you disagree, but you also have a ready-made project management tool for the job. You just need to turn it into a social/emotional intelligence tool as well.

Use a risk analysis or assessment when you're told to do something that whispers to you of impending disaster. You can use the usual types of format. Start with the problem—the decision you've been handed. Note the risks and benefits you see with the path you'll be following (be sure to come up with a few benefits). Give the other options that you see that might be better ways to resolve the issue or question that resulted in the decision. Explain each option and note the risks and benefits of each. Finally, give your recommendation on the course of action using the risks and benefits you've seen.

If you do this in the same format every time and use it sparingly, you'll usually find that your manager is going to pay attention to what you're saying. People one step removed from the project often can't see all the possible risks and may not be able to formulate other options, so you're providing valuable information that may not be at your manager's immediate disposal. With any luck, your manager will follow your recommendation. If not, she probably has information not available to you that's driving the decision, so don't take it personally if the decision doesn't change.

All this means that you've provided information in a recognizable and easily digestible format, and you aren't directly questioning a decision (which might result in some side effects you won't enjoy). Your manager should in any case be pleased to have more information even if it doesn't change the decision, and it makes the risks clear. It also puts you and your team a bit ahead of the game because you've identified risks that you'll need to analyze further, no matter which option is chosen.

When you put the analysis together, involve your team if you can do so without amping them up, revealing confidential information, or setting unrealistic expectations. You may get additional options you hadn't considered and more information on possible risks and benefits. You're also helping your team bond over shared problem-solving, trusting them with the information about the decision and your next steps.

Risk analysis is a powerful tool in many situations, and from a communication perspective it's businesslike and fairly apolitical.

USE RETROSPECTIVES TO CONNECT THE DOTS

I've talked a bit about retrospectives/postmortems to help keep bad things from recurring and to help identify things that are working well. Their use can go far beyond just end-of-project wrap-ups and follow-up on critical situations.

Postmortems/retrospectives can be used for everything from a milestone analysis to your own end-of-year review and planning. Once you get in the habit it becomes almost automatic. (I use them for everything from analyzing reviews of classes and presentations to figuring out why a phone call didn't go well.) They're great for implementing continuous improvement—the more you have them, the more data you have on what went well and whether previous improvements and process changes did what they were meant to do.

If you do them regularly and consistently, these reviews will show you patterns of process, behavior, and data that can help you hone your processes as well as your people skills. Traditionally in project management, they've been used to review processes, but if you use retrospectives in nontraditional situations, they can help you understand when and under what circumstances communications go well (or not so well). Go ahead and try it. Next time you're in a meeting that ends in a shouting match (whether it was your meeting or not and whether you were a shouter or not), try to figure out what led to that end and how you might keep it from happening again. At the other end of the spectrum, next time you have a really good meeting, try to figure out what made it so good and how you can repeat it.

This will work well with all kinds of things with your team. You don't have to call it a retrospective or postmortem, just ask the questions in a regular meeting, either with your team or in a one-on-one. You'll get a broader view of everyday activities, good suggestions on how things can generally be improved, and a team engaged in the process as well as the product.

METRICS AND MEASUREMENTS

It seems like metrics and measurements don't really belong in a book about social and emotional intelligence, but there's a surprising amount of interplay between what you measure and what your team does.

There was a time at the height of the Six Sigma craze when the corporate mantra was "pick something, anything, and measure it." Bad idea, as it turns out.

Measurements drive behavior. How could they not? You're focusing on an aspect of your team's daily lives, which means that it's an important aspect or that it's a problem or both. People will respond to measurements and work to improve them, which is a good thing—within limits. The problem is that there are side effects of any measurement that need to be carefully considered.

Here's an example. Let's say you're running a Customer Support team. Wait times are rising, which makes customers unhappy. Your budget is limited with respect to being able to hire more support representatives, and you know you'll need ammunition if you're going to go forward with a request for more representatives. You start to measure call time—how long does it take a support representative to resolve a problem? You're surprised by the average time of a call and believe it's too long. Pretty soon you're posting the metrics about call time and people are paying attention. They can tell it's a problem and, more importantly, believe that they'll be evaluated on their own call times. You're happy to see the call times start to drop, but now you have unhappy customers because they're calling in multiple times to get a problem resolved. Why? Because your support reps are trying to get customers off the phone as quickly as possible so their numbers are good. How do you find the balance for this? It's easier than you think. You just have to have a second balancing measurement, like number of times a customer has to call to get an issue resolved or customer satisfaction with issue resolution. Measuring too many things will defeat the purpose of the measurements by splitting focus and making it difficult for your team to understand what's most important, but two balancing measurements will help them see the bigger picture. People are smart. They will strike a balance if you give them the two sides of the equation.

You yourself might be looking at many measurements, even publishing them, but you'll want to focus on just a few with your team to keep everyone moving in the same direction (goals again!).

While this isn't a book on measurements, I can give you a fairly simple way to get started with the right ones. First, look at the goals you're trying to achieve. (Hint: If you don't know what the goals are, you need to find out or establish them, or you'll never know what to measure or when you're done.) Once you know your goals, think about whether you're meeting them. Whatever you're using to evaluate whether you're meeting your goals in the first place is probably going to be your best measurement to start with (in other words, how did you know your customers were unhappy?). Once you establish that measurement, think ahead. What could people do to improve the measurement that wouldn't be a good thing? (For example, getting customers off the phone faster even if their problems aren't resolved.) However you measure that response will be your balancing measure (are the customers' problems actually resolved, for example). The main caution is to be sure you don't trap your team in a place where they can't find the right thing to do. As always, present the information for feedback from your team before you implement the measurements—if given the chance, they will tell you what the pitfalls will be. Even better, involve them in developing the measurements to begin with, using the skills you've developed in getting feedback and using the team synergy to achieve a better result.

CONCLUSION

Wrap It Up

Early in my career I took a class on giving presentations. One technique that stuck with me was that any presentation should have three parts:

1. Tell them what you're going to tell them.
2. Tell them.
3. Tell them what you told them.

I use this for presentations, classes, meetings, you name it. We're at that third step now, so let's wrap this up with some summaries and conclusions.

Let's follow it like a flowchart. (In fact, I'll update the introduction's flowchart at the end in figure 2!)

WHY BOTHER

Project management is all about accomplishing tasks through people. If you love the people part of the equation, I hope this book has given you new tools and ideas to explore to pursue that passion. If you're not so fond of the people part but love the process and order of a schedule, you should be realizing that one unhappy person can ruin your beautiful plan and send your project into chaos, so you need to keep your people happy. The tools I've given you will help you make more of a process out of the people side and will keep your plan in order and your process moving smoothly.

RELATIONSHIPS

Establishing relationships with individuals on and associated with your team is the first and most critical step in building a strong people game. Relationships need to be built one-on-one and starting from scratch, and they need to be maintained regularly. Yes, it's time consuming; yes, it's like nailing Jell-O to a tree; and yes, it's important.

MOTIVATION

Lack of motivation is contagious—it will spread from one unmotivated person on your team to the rest of your team, and you'll have trouble maintaining your plan and schedules. You have to do your research to understand what motivates each person on your team and work to keep each person motivated throughout the project. Unless you have a relationship with an individual, it's difficult to really uncover motivation (so start with the relationship). You need to dig a bit—ask the right questions as well as observing behavior.

LEARNING STYLES AND OTHER PROFILES

There are five different learning styles that translate to communication styles. Everyone can use all the styles to process information, but we all have so much information being thrown at us on a daily basis that most people will use their most comfortable style first. Understanding and using each person's favorite communication style will help keep you at the top of her list when you need her attention. Even when you're communicating to large groups of people you can easily tailor that communication (presentations, minutes, reports) so that it appeals to the largest number of people at once in the same communication. There are other kinds of profiles, like the Myers-Briggs personality inventory, that can give you and your team insight into what makes individuals tick, but use them sparingly and cautiously so you don't start treating people like categories.

MEETINGS AND MINUTES

Project managers spend a lot of time in meetings and should be spending time documenting those meetings in minutes. No one likes meetings that drag on and take people away from their work, but if you follow a few simple guidelines, you can get people to your meetings on time and get them to read your minutes regularly.

Meeting rules:

- Send an agenda the day before and include action items.
- Bring a few printed copies of the agenda.
- Invite the right people.
- Start and end on time.
- Cater to learning styles.
- Videoconference when you can if everyone isn't at the same location.

Minutes rules:

- Always provide minutes of your meetings within 24 hours.
- Start with a list of who was there.
- Summarize.
- Use outline form.
- Put decisions near the top.

- List action items including those just closed.
- Put the text of the minutes into emails (don't just attach them or provide a link).

NO-PANIC EMERGENCY RESPONSES

The first thing to do when a problem occurs is to not panic.

The second thing to do is to get everyone together who might take adrenaline-fueled action (making things worse) and come up with a plan or trigger an existing contingency plan. Make it clear who will do what, when they'll report, and how you'll keep everyone in the loop.

And the third thing to do is keep everyone from trying to figure out *who* is responsible and get them worrying about *what* caused the problem and *how* to fix it.

Do root cause analysis if the problem is a nasty surprise, with the right people in the room with the right tools.

Fix the problem.

Celebrate your success.

After your team stands down and everyone has a chance to recover and eat some chocolate, have a postmortem to better understand why the problem happened and how to keep it from happening again. Always investigate what went right as part of this—you want to keep doing the good things as much as you want to avoid the bad ones.

WORK WITH YOUR TEAM'S PERSONALITY

Every team has its own personality and its own identity. Help them find it, and reinforce the identity every chance you get.

Build your team with soft skills in mind as well as hard skills. If you're missing critical soft skills, work as hard to develop or acquire them as you would if you were missing an irreplaceable technical skill.

Create, evangelize, and track the project goals. Be sure that everyone has the same understanding of them and that everyone knows how he or she contributes to meeting the goals.

If your team isn't sitting all together, as teams often aren't these days, you'll need to work extra hard to include everyone. Use videoconferencing, travel when possible, and distribute critical tasks across all locations.

Understand the personality of other teams critical to the success of your project, and ensure that your team has continuing good relations with those other teams.

Finally, look for signs that your team is turning toxic, and catch it early on. You can do a lot of ground work to keep that from happening at all, and if it does show up, your best chance is to recognize it early and deal with it.

BUILD AND CELEBRATE

Now you have a team with an identity working together with other teams. You have all the skills you need to have a successful project. But like relationships, your team's well-being needs to be both built *and* maintained.

Work on team building, both the bigger team-building exercises and the small day-to-day things that help the team remain cohesive and committed to the effort. Use technology in your efforts, especially if you have a geographically distributed team.

Be sure that all the assignments are specific. Never assign a task to "the team." If there's more than one person who is needed to contribute to a task, assign a person as the lead.

Pay attention to any disparity between a team member's skill and his or her own perception of that skill level; accurate self-perception with respect to skills is essential to working well with the rest of the team and completing the project work.

Celebrate often. Milestones and end-of-project celebrations are great, but work on celebrating small steps and achievements as often as you can.

WORK WITH DIVERSITY IN LOCATION AND CULTURE

Culture is defined by more than just country. Everything from religion to company to region to education can carry cultural implications that you need to work with.

Learn to recognize the different types of culture at work on your team and among the other teams that contribute to your project. Don't be afraid to ask questions, but definitely do your homework. Cultural intelligence is an emerging field, but the definitions agree on three elements:

1. Head—do your research and go in ready to observe.
2. Hands—understand and participate in physical gestures and activities appropriate to the culture.
3. Heart—believe that you can learn about other cultures and be proficient in them.

FEED YOUR TEAM

Food is the common denominator in all cultures. Sharing food means sharing information. Food can get people to meetings, get them talking, and get you valuable information about the state of your project. Even getting a cup of coffee usually means interesting and open conversation that helps establish and maintain relationships. Use food wisely (and often) in your projects to help build and maintain the team, get people to take a break (or keep on working), and get information about how the project is really going.

BALANCE

There are really three parts to any project:

1. Product—what the project is meant to build or achieve
2. Process—how you build the product, keep on track, and keep everyone moving in the same direction
3. People—getting the work done successfully through the members of the project team and associated teams

All three are critical. Without the product need, there's no need for the team. Without process, you have no road map or guidelines and it's difficult to manage the work. And without people, there is no way to produce the product. Your job as the project manager is to balance these three critical pieces to successfully complete your project.

You will also need to balance the needs of your team with the needs of your management, providing the right (and right amount of) information to each.

VOLUNTEERS

Volunteers are a special case of social and emotional intelligence. They need to be managed a little differently and with great attention, or you'll find yourself without a team at all.

Uncover motivations as fast as possible. The direct way—asking—usually works pretty well with volunteers, but keep an eye on them along the way. If a volunteer isn't getting what she wants out of a volunteer experience, she'll walk away.

Realize that each member of a volunteer team comes to the team with a different background, methods, and expectations. Sometimes these differences are extreme. You'll want to cater to everyone as much as possible, which may mean coming up with creative processes that satisfy your volunteers.

Communicate constantly, realizing that time and attention span of volunteers are usually much shorter than those of a work or professional team. Find the channels that appeal to your volunteers and keep communications brief. (More frequent is much better than longer communications.)

GO GET 'EM

So there you have it. You have all the tools you need to navigate the murky world of people and teams and some good processes to help put you on a more comfortable footing.

Remember that people are the heart of your team, not an afterthought. Treat them well, fairly, and openly, and you'll have teams that love working together.

THE FLOW

Now that you've followed all the steps, here's how they look (figure 2):

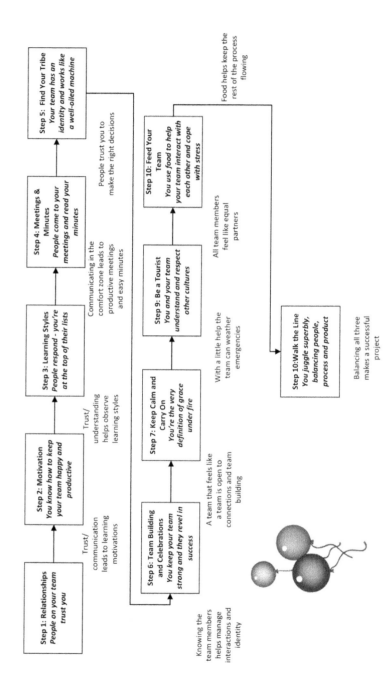

Figure 2 Success! A Look Back at the Road to Emotional/Social Intelligence

NOTES

Introduction

1. Wikipedia, s.v. "Emotional Intelligence," last modified May 22, 2019, https://en.wikipedia.org/wiki/Emotional_intelligence.

Step 2

1. For more information on motivation cards, see the Management 3.0 website at https://management30.com/practice/.

2. Stevie Wilson, "The Biology of Play," accessed July 17, 2019, http://www.steviewilsonlpc.com/the-biology-of-play/.

3. Phys.org, "Job Satisfaction Not a Persistent Effect of Wage Increases," https://phys.org/news/2018-02-job-satisfaction-persistent-effect-wage.html.

Step 5

1. Tom DeMarco and Timothy Lister, *Peopleware* (Crawfordsville, IN: Addison-Wesley, 2013), 146.

Step 9

1. Anne Fishel, "The Most Important Thing You Can Do with Your Kids? Eat Dinner with Them," *Washington Post*, January 12, 2015, https://www.washingtonpost.com/posteverything/wp/2015/01

/12/the-most-important-thing-you-can-do-with-your-kids-eat
-dinner-with-them/?utm_term=.2ac64cfbdbef.

2. Shankar Vedantam, "Why Eating the Same Food Increases
People's Trust and Cooperation," *Morning Edition*, February 2, 2017,
https://www.npr.org/2017/02/02/512998465/why-eating-the-same
-food-increases-peoples-trust-and-cooperation.

3. Fran Kritz, "You Say Chocolate Relieves Your Stress? Now Science Provides Some Backup," Everyday Health, October 16, 2018,
https://www.everydayhealth.com/wellness/united-states-of-stress
/you-say-chocolate-relieves-your-stress-now-science-provides-some
-back-up/.

REFERENCES

Cialdini, Robert B. *Influence: Science and Practice.* Needham Heights, MA: Allyn & Bacon, 2001.

DeMarco, Tom, and Timothy Lister. *Peopleware: Productive Projects and Teams.* Crawfordsville, IN: Addison Wesley, 2013.

Early, P. Christopher, and E. Mosakowski. "Cultural Intelligence." *Harvard Business Review,* October 2004.

Goleman, Daniel. *Emotional Intelligence: Why It Can Matter More Than IQ.* New York: Bantam Dell, 2005.

Goleman, Daniel. *Social Intelligence: The Revolutionary New Science of Human Relationships.* New York: Bantam Dell, 2006.

The Myers & Briggs Foundation. "MBTI Basics." MBTI. https://www.myersbriggs.org/my-mbti-personality-type/mbti-basics/home.htm?bhcp=1.

ACKNOWLEDGMENTS

This book would not have been possible without a tribe of people backing me up.

Many thanks to my husband, Tris, and extended family (Ceili Wasson, Micki Hahn, Jan Alderson, Donette Dake, Scott Hellewell) for both their encouragement and their patience. They gave me the space and the cheerleading to get the book written.

Special thanks to my brother-in-law Stephen for providing the amazing illustrations. He did it all from chapter titles and captured the spirit of each one with the cats to herd. Because of him, the visual learners get something to hang their hats on and all of us get a chuckle.

Without my business coach Julie Foucht I never would have found the path to the book, and I am forever indebted to her for that and all other things marketing.

My editor, Charlotte Ashlock, found me and helped me through the processes of proposal, structuring, getting ready for publication, and all the other things that go along with being a neophyte author. She spent countless hours brainstorming and encouraging, and went to bat for me big time to get approval. Without her, there would have been no book.

My expert reviewers Deb Kelly, Patti Gosselin, and Bruce Gay did an amazing job reviewing the book, pointing out what spoke to them and providing many excellent suggestions that made the final version so much better than the first draft.

Mentors throughout my career helped me learn how to do this job right, from Keith Jenkins, Hattie Donovan, Dave Stroh, Jim Allen, and Arlene Dolci at IBM; to Wendy Held, Angela Spearman, and Chris Melville at SCO; to Martin McKendry at Resumix and beyond, every one of them showed me by example and advice how to do this job right. Michele Jackman was an inspiration in the areas of humor in business and toxic team management. Obviously, Daniel Goleman's research and writing on both social and emotional intelligence helped me put my experiences into a well-researched framework.

My horse Jenn taught me how to listen and all about making it easier to do the right thing than the wrong thing, which lessons carried through to people, dogs, cats, and probably lizards and birds (although I haven't yet tried the last two).

And finally, of course, many, many thanks to Berrett-Koehler and the entire staff for doing such an incredible job bringing my book to life.

INDEX

ABOUT THE AUTHOR

 Kim Wasson has spent more time than she cares to think about in the software industry. Starting with a Computer Science degree from California State University, Chico, she got a solid grounding in software development, project management, and management from IBM before moving to increasingly smaller and more interesting Silicon Valley start-ups. Partway through, she picked up a Master's Degree from Stanford University in Industrial Engineering and Engineering Management (renamed to the infinitely more digestible Management Science and Engineering the day after graduation). After a stint with eBay managing project managers, she struck out on her own with a consulting firm, IvyBay Consulting LLC.

Over the years Kim has worked as a programmer, systems and procedures analyst, quality engineer, project manager, program manager, and in management from line manager through the VP level. Thanks to an engineer in a start-up who had worked on the original eXtreme Programming team, she had an early introduction to Agile development and has practiced the process stand-alone and in hybrid models ever since. As a consultant she's taken on roles in all facets of software development and operations, adding coaching and teaching to her repertoire. Kim earned her PMP certification to better help coach clients through their own PMP journeys.

Kim found her voice advocating people skills in project management after starting IvyBay. She's presented at the PMI Global Conference multiple times on the topic and continues to seek out research to support her personal experience in the application of emotional/social intelligence in project management with empirical data.

Berrett–Koehler
Publishers

Berrett-Koehler is an independent publisher dedicated to an ambitious mission: *Connecting people and ideas to create a world that works for all.*

Our publications span many formats, including print, digital, audio, and video. We also offer online resources, training, and gatherings. And we will continue expanding our products and services to advance our mission.

We believe that the solutions to the world's problems will come from all of us, working at all levels: in our society, in our organizations, and in our own lives. Our publications and resources offer pathways to creating a more just, equitable, and sustainable society. They help people make their organizations more humane, democratic, diverse, and effective (and we don't think there's any contradiction there). And they guide people in creating positive change in their own lives and aligning their personal practices with their aspirations for a better world.

And we strive to practice what we preach through what we call "The BK Way." At the core of this approach is *stewardship*, a deep sense of responsibility to administer the company for the benefit of all of our stakeholder groups, including authors, customers, employees, investors, service providers, sales partners, and the communities and environment around us. Everything we do is built around stewardship and our other core values of *quality, partnership, inclusion,* and *sustainability.*

This is why Berrett-Koehler is the first book publishing company to be both a B Corporation (a rigorous certification) and a benefit corporation (a for-profit legal status), which together require us to adhere to the highest standards for corporate, social, and environmental performance. And it is why we have instituted many pioneering practices (which you can learn about at www.bkconnection.com), including the Berrett-Koehler Constitution, the Bill of Rights and Responsibilities for BK Authors, and our unique Author Days.

We are grateful to our readers, authors, and other friends who are supporting our mission. We ask you to share with us examples of how BK publications and resources are making a difference in your lives, organizations, and communities at www.bkconnection.com/impact.

Dear reader,

Thank you for picking up this book and welcome to the worldwide BK community! You're joining a special group of people who have come together to create positive change in their lives, organizations, and communities.

What's BK all about?

Our mission is to connect people and ideas to create a world that works for all.

Why? Our communities, organizations, and lives get bogged down by old paradigms of self-interest, exclusion, hierarchy, and privilege. But we believe that can change. That's why we seek the leading experts on these challenges—and share their actionable ideas with you.

A welcome gift

To help you get started, we'd like to offer you a **free copy** of one of our bestselling ebooks:

www.bkconnection.com/welcome

When you claim your **free ebook**, you'll also be subscribed to our blog.

Our freshest insights

Access the best new tools and ideas for leaders at all levels on our blog at ideas.bkconnection.com.

Sincerely,

Your friends at Berrett-Koehler